Answering The Call

Chad McCrary

Authored with:

Nick LaToof

All photos and text remain the property of Chad McCrary. Photos that belong to other entities are given credit where such credit is deserved. Direct quotes are accredited to the author. In the case where more than one author may be accredited, we have quoted the author whom was found first and/or in the context that is best useful for this book.

ANSWERING THE CALL: Copyright © 2017 by Chad McCrary and Nick LaToof. All rights reserved. No part of this book may be used or reproduced in any manner whatsoever without the express written consent of Chad McCrary. Exceptions include brief quotations embodied in critical articles and/or reviews. Criminal charges may be pursued by Chad or any other affiliates if unlawful use or misrepresentation of this book has been discovered.

A portion of this book's profits will go toward the Christopher and Dana Reeve Foundation in support of spinal cord research. Their logos and trademarks belong to them. The Christopher and Dana Reeve foundation do not necessarily endorse or stand behind the views, expressions, and/or opinions of Chad McCrary from the past or in the future.

This book has been funded by Chad McCrary. No other funding was raised. There are no other entities that receive proceeds from the book except for the following: CreateSpace, Amazon.com, The Christopher and Dana Reeve Foundation, Nick LaToof, and Chad McCrary.

ANSWERING THE CALL
Copyright © 2017
ISBN-13: 978-1981498383
ISBN10: 1981498389

DEDICATION

God
Your plan has always been better than mine. Thank you for not giving up on me and using my struggle to empower others.

Jon Minter & Bruce Bryant
Two of the best workout partners I've ever had. You guys are much more than lifting buddies. Y'all are friends and brothers. I'd do anything for you two. Thank you for your encouragement and support. You push me to be better every day.

Amanda
I will always be thankful for support and encouragement; it has been a tremendous blessing.

To all who have stood by my side and voiced their support. The list is far too long to share here. I can't thank you enough. Without you, I wouldn't be where I am today. I dedicate this book for all of you… past, present, and future.

Message from the Writer
Nick LaToof

To the reader:

I feel incredibly blessed to have helped Chad with this project. I believe that it will have a positive impact on whoever reads it. Chad's story is powerful and his message is life changing. Hearing Chad share his story, first hand, has definitely impacted me. The small things I sometimes complain about fail in comparison to what Chad has overcome. I believe we all can learn and grow from Chad's story.

Each phone conversation we had turned into a motivational speech from the both of us. I left each conversation more and more excited about the book and life. If you're fortunate enough to know Chad, you know that he is a world-class dude, willing to help you out with anything. Chad once drove me to the DFW airport from DeKalb at 4:00 AM. That's about a two and half-hour trip. Chad never hesitated when I asked him. You'd be hard-pressed to find another guy as genuine and caring as Chad McCrary. If you have a friend half as cool as Chad, I'd consider you to be very lucky. I consider it an honor and a blessing to count him among my friends.

To Chad,

I can't thank you enough for allowing me to work with you on this project. I'm convinced that this book will do big things and that your message will change the lives of all who hear it. But, more importantly, thanks for being a friend. The world needs more people like you.

CONTENTS

Acknowledgments

Intro — xv

1. Small Town Kid — 1
2. The Hustle — 12
3. Life as a Paramedic — 23
4. Building the Body — 31
5. Flying High — 39
6. Clouds & Dirt — 57
7. Plan the Flight Fly the Plan. — 67
8. From a Chair — 79
9. The Dark Times — 89
10. One Final Recovery — 97
11. Back on Stage — 101
12. Answering the Call — 111
13. Overcoming Adversity — 121

Author Bio's & Other — 127

ACKNOWLEDGMENTS

SPECIAL THANKS TO:

Nick LaToof

Without you, this book wouldn't have been possible. I can't express enough how much I appreciate your dedication to this project and your friendship.

Christopher and Dana Reeve Foundation

What you've done for spinal cord research has been tremendous. Without your devotion and selflessness, many would be unnecessarily struggling with injuries. I'm proud to help further support spinal cord research by donating a percentage of the proceeds from this book. Thank you for your support.

It's dark. I find myself lying face down. The only thing keeping my face from resting on the dirt is a helmet.

"My helmet?!" I thought to myself.

I lifted my head to see several pair of boots walking around me. These boots belonged to friends and other riders who had been with me all day at the track.

For a brief moment, I'm confused, very confused.

My gaze then turns to a lonely pair of boots, sitting neatly a few feet away… they sat there alone… in the dirt… still among the ciaos.

I felt like I only existed from the waist up. I tried pushing myself up but nothing happened.

"Chad. Chad! Get up!"

"I can't man…" I responded in anguish.

"Chad, come on dude. Get up."

Answering The Call

CHAPTER ONE

"Small Town Kid"

There were many things I wished to do as a kid. Most were completely out of the question. Growing up in a small town you learn to do without things that aren't completely necessary. You learn about things that are far more important than material possessions. Things like hard work, discipline and respect. There was nothing special about growing up in DeKalb, TX. The small town offered very little for the curious or ambitious. Luckily, for me, I wasn't an overly ambitious kid. I found enough there to get into and satisfy my youthful appetite for fun and adventure.

My father, Ronny McCrary, had moved to Fort Worth, TX to work for Texas Instruments. You know, the calculator company. While there, he met my mother, Linda Mantooth. Her ancestors were of Native American decent, Cherokee if my memory serves me right. She fell in love with my father and got married. Not long after they were married they started a family when my oldest brother, Lance, was born. I would make my entrance to this world three and half years later.

I was born on April 1, 1974 at Fort Worth Methodist Hospital. My stay, along with my family's, in Fort Worth would be short lived. We moved to my hometown of DeKalb, TX not long after I was born. My grandfather, on my dad's side, owned a car dealership there. McCray Auto Sales it was called. My father would help my grandfather with the day-to-day operations.

I can remember many days where Lance and I would run through the show room of freshly made, newly shined Chevy trucks. McCrary Auto Sales was quite successful and known throughout Bowie County. Although many thought it to be just a rumor, my grandfather grossed over one million dollars between the mid sixties and seventies.

A million dollars was large chunk of change for a small town like DeKalb. My reasoning for sharing is not to brag or boastful in nature. Rather, it shows you what hard work and honesty can do. That type of success doesn't come from taking short cuts or taking advantage of people. I think it speaks volumes about my grandfather and the type of guy he was. Success like that requires discipline and hard work, two things my grandfather never shied away from. My grandfather was as reliable as the summer days are long. A handshake with him was as good as a guarantee.

I learned a lot from my grandfather. He taught me honesty, respect, reliability, and what an honest day's work would get you. My grandparents played a significant role in raising me. I spent countless hours at their house and dozens of memories are sketched into my mind. My mother and father didn't get along to well. My mother left when I was nine years old and our relationship would be pretty rocky until the day she died.

My father remarried when I was fifteen years old. I was a freshman in high school and had a brand new, half sister named Lauren. We connected immediately and got along very well. We've remained close throughout the years. Lauren has supported me and been by my side during my darkest days. She's one of those people who enter your life, unexpectedly, and makes you wonder what life was like without them.

My father was a great man and worked extremely hard, much like my grandfather. Growing up I didn't get to spend a lot of time with him. The dealership required most of my dad's time so he was always there. He brought Lance and I to work with him when he could somewhat afford the distraction. Lance and I couldn't help but get into trouble at the dealership so I don't blame my father for not bringing us more often.

My grandfather worked in the dealership for decades. When my father joined, my grandfather took a step back and allowed my father to handle the majority of the day-to-day operations. In his semi-retired state, my grandfather would help fill the void of my father's absence. My grandfather was the oldest child in his family. When his father passed, he became the man of the house, at the ripe-old age of thirteen. I remember him telling me stories of how hard he had to work. You know, the "uphill both ways" kind of stories. I didn't appreciate them quite as much as I do now.

We shared many great memories together. One of my fondest memories I have with my grandfather is one that brings a smile to my face, as I recollect. My grandparents had an old cabin down by the Red River. Naturally, we all called it the "River Place." My grandfather would go there to work on countless unfinished projects. I'm sure it also served as an escape from the normal hustle of everyday life.

It was junky and disorganized. Tools and used car parts were scattered through the grasses, of varying heights. It would be difficult to keep the grass at the same length, as mowing would be a constant game of avoiding all the scrap metal and used car parts. When the grass grew obnoxiously high, my grandfather would weed-eat between the scraps of junk, making it a bit more presentable, in a junkyard kind of way.

The fact that it was so junky and more or less of a man's place, was more than enough reason for my grandmother to decline the majority of invitations to go. I can only recall a few instances where she joined us. I don't believe my grandfather blamed here for not tagging along. I often accompanied him down to the River Place. He never desired to go alone and many times he would let me drive.

It was a much different time, growing up in the eighties. Folks didn't think much of a ten year old driving from the farm to the market. After all, the cars and trucks back then didn't go near as fast as they do now. The roads weren't nearly as dangerous. One afternoon, I was playing out in the yard and I hear my grandfather, "Hey Chad!" he yelled.

"Let's run down to the River Place. I'll let you drive!"

A big grin came to my face as I heard my grandfather's words. I ran as fast as I could to meet my grandfather on the front porch. I would usually have to do a bit of persuading in order for him to let me drive but this time it was offered freely. No way was I going to allow this opportunity to pass.

Earlier that day, I had befriended a stray cat and it had taken quite a liking to me. I decided that the cat would come with my grandfather and I. We all loaded up in the truck and everything was smooth sailing. Until, that is, the cat went crazy. To this day, I have no idea what came over that cat. It totally flipped out.

I swerved all over the one lane country road, going into both ditches and knocking off both side mirrors. The cat was bouncing all over the cab, like a pinball. It jumped from the dash to the back window and both side windows. Finally, my grandfather was able to get the cat out the window. I managed to bring the truck to a stop in the middle of the dirt road.

Both our hearts were pounding inside our chests and heavy breathing filled the air. We sat there for a few moments. The truck had a ringing silence to it, like a gun had gone off between us. Eventually, I turned to look to my grandfather, worried that he'd be furious with me. He looked at me and between breaths said, "Damn boy, your grandmother told me not to let you drive!"

He cracked a smile and it turned into a light laugh. A smile came to my face and then I laughed in relief. The truck had taken quite a beating but the important thing was that we were both safe and unharmed. My grandfather was slow to anger and always had a good outlook on what really mattered.

Life sure is funny and boy, has it changed significantly over the years. Today, as I worked with Nick on this book project, I took a mental note. I reminded myself that it's important to stop, take a look around, and appreciate all that you have, and everything that's happened in the past. Don't waste time worrying about things you can't change or control. Focus on what you can control and give it your all. There's one thing that is guaranteed in this life: you've only got one shot, so make it count.

I enjoyed high school, probably a little too much. I never took my schoolwork seriously. For me, school was a place to hang out with my buddies. During the week, we would decide on our plan for the upcoming weekend. I did just what was necessary to get by. My only goal was to graduate. As long as I did that, I was cool with whatever.

I wasn't much of an athlete, either. I played football my freshman year but quickly learned that it wasn't for me. Each practice I did my fair share of push-ups. I would have to push myself up off the ground after getting knocked down. My scrawny butt wasn't made for football. As a senior, I played left field for the baseball team but that quickly sums up my high school athletic career. It's not that I wouldn't consider myself an athlete. My lack of participation stemmed mainly from a lack of motivation. I simply didn't want to play. The desire was just not there. I was much more concerned with what was happening on Friday and Saturday night.

I do my best not to look back on life with regret. At times, however, I do look back on my high school years and wish I would've taken things more seriously. I could go back and forth and play the hypothetical game all day but that wouldn't change anything. I believe that everything happens for a reason and that regrets are a big waste of time. But, you'll definitely not hear me encourage others to do what I did in high school.

A Pivotal Moment

After high school, I worked construction for a few years. I had my father and grandfathers work ethic and I enjoyed the manual labor. Like most kids fresh out of high school, I hadn't given much thought to my future. I knew that I wouldn't be doing construction forever but I continued to put off thinking about what I'd do with my life.

One particular day, around quitting time, I found myself back at my buddy's truck. I got there before he did so I dropped the tailgate and waited for him. As I waited, I noticed the older guys, of our crew, returning to their vehicles. Years of construction and the Texas heat had clearly taken its toll. These guys looked tired and beaten down. They looked forward to quitting time each day; grateful that they had survived another workday and that they were one day closer to the weekend.

I respected the hell out of these guys. They were hard workers and trustworthy dudes but I just couldn't see myself in their shoes twenty years from now. I knew that I would need to make a change or before I knew it, I'd be one of the older guys wondering where the hell my life had gone. I felt a conviction so strong that it brought tears to my eyes.

I was born for more than this; I was selling myself too short.

My buddy finally made it back to the truck. I knew he could tell that I was a bit shaken up but he didn't say a word. We loaded up the truck and hit the road. The truck remained silent, dead silent, all the way home. My mind raced 100 miles per hour. I needed to do something and quick. I wasn't exactly sure of what lay ahead but I knew that it was a road worth taking.

CHAPTER TWO

"The Hustle"

"I think I know what I'm gonna do."

"Well, what's that?" my buddy responded.

"I want to be a paramedic." I said confidently.

My buddy laughed. His reaction didn't surprise me. He had good reason to laugh. To become a paramedic required a ton of schooling and with my educational history, it seemed like a lost cause. Up until this point, I lived my life one-quarter mile at a time. I never paid too much attention to my future or where I was going. If I was going to pull this off, and make something of myself, I'd have to get my act together.

My alarm clock sounds around 4:00 A.M. I debate on hitting the snooze button. Simultaneously, I consider if all this is going to be worth it. I don't allow myself to contemplate these thoughts for long. I know the longer they linger the more likely I am to fall vitcim to their temptation. So, I turn off the alarm and get up. I won't be doing this forever, I convince myself.

I prepare my things for the day and then make my way to work. Currently, we are working construction on a church in Hope, AR. It's a solid hour and a half drive from DeKalb. The drive allotted plenty of time to think and ponder. Each morning and afternoon, I would convince myself that I wouldn't be doing this forever and that each day was getting me closer to where I wanted to be. I just needed to suck it up and get through it.

I would arrive in Hope only to be greeted by a ten-hour workday, with a half hour lunch break. When quitting time came around, I did by best not to delay. My day was far from over. In fact, in many cases, it was just beginning. I would get back to my old Ford Zephyr, a former driver's education car. The "Blue Bomb" I called it. It was a junky ole thing but it got me where I needed to go with decent reliability. I told myself that I would buy a nice car once I began working as a paramedic and firefighter. I dreamed of driving an old muscle car, possibly even a convertible.

I would get back home as quickly as I could. I would hop in the shower, change clothes, and grab a bite to eat, if time allowed. Then, I'd jump back in the Blue Bomb and hit the road to Mount Pleasant, for night classes. Northeast Texas Community College (NTCC) had a program with all the classes

I would need. It was local and affordable; it would be my ticket to a better life.

It was quite intimidating, going to college. I didn't know what to expect. I had assumed that it would be much harder than high school. I didn't exactly take the hard classes in high school. In fact, I put forth such little effort that the teachers elected to put me in the special education program. This is something that few know about me; and, I'm not real proud of it. I didn't care about school back then. All I wanted to do was graduate and that's what I did. I found the path of least resistance and accomplished my goal.

I had no choice but to face my fear and doubt head on. I had to overcome the obstacles and adversity. I knew exactly what would happen if I didn't try, nothing. If I tried and couldn't quite make it, I'd be disappointed, for sure. But, I could live with that outcome. I couldn't live with not trying. Nothing was going to change if I didn't make a conscious effort to do so. At the very least, if I tried and failed, I'd have my answer, as humbling and devastating as it may be.

I took some entry-level tests in order for the college to determine where I should start. I passed all these tests with ease; it came as no surprise to me. I don't think anybody assumed that I was stupid, lazy perhaps, but not stupid. Like I said, I had a genuine disinterest for education in high school. I cruised right through the pre-requisites at NTCC. Before I knew it, I was in legit emergency medicine technician (EMT) classes.

I quickly found a passion and a strong interest in the

subject matter. I surprised myself about how fascinated I was by learning all the intricate details of the human body. I became so emerged in my studies that my friends had stopped coming around. The more information I learned, the more I wanted to know. I had become "book nerd Chad." I did my best to soak up everything in my textbooks, as well as in class.

My days were long and exhausting. I had little free time to party with my friends, even if I had wanted to. The weekends had become a time for me to catch up or get ahead on my studies along with resting up for another grueling week of hustle. Every free moment I had I utilized it to study. To my surprise, I didn't really miss the weekend parties. The sense of fulfillment I got bettering myself through education was far beyond what I could've imagined. I was addicted.

I knew that each step I took brought me closer to my ultimate goal. If that meant I had to put aside the weekend parties and hanging out with friends, I was okay with that. I knew I didn't want to work construction my whole life. I had finally found something that I cared about and developed a passion for. When I started out, I knew that there would be sacrifices I would have to make. Albeit very difficult, I was willing to do what was necessary to be successful. I had no problem sacrificing my today for a better tomorrow.

Slowly, I drifted away from my group of friends that I had hung out with for years. We had a ton of good times and shared many great memories. But, for me, it was time to move on. I couldn't afford to have anything hold me back. I was laser focused on what I needed to do. I couldn't afford to have any distractions.

To this day, I keep a very small circle of friends. I prefer it this way. These friends are people I can trust, no matter what. I seek them for advice and comfort in times of pain or struggle. I know that if I ever called upon one of them, they'd be there for me, as I would for them.

That's one of the things that makes success hard. Sometimes, you have to let go of things you've always know, that have always been a part of your life. Many people aren't willing to let go. They are unable to leave their friends or family and *just go*. Despite the overwhelming conviction to do so, most refuse to take that leap of faith. There's no doubt that it's a difficult thing to do. But, if you're going to continue to dream about it, and desire it, why not just go after it? You'll get called crazy, sure. You'll be lucky if that's the worst thing you are called. That's just part of it. The ones that call you crazy will be the ones who sing you praises once you've conquered your goal. It's your vision; don't expect others to see it. Make it your mission to show them, by doing it.

My friends weren't doing anything wrong. They were young and just wanted to have a good time. I was the same way until I desired something different. I'm not better than them or anybody else because I chose to change my course. I wanted something and knew that my current path wouldn't get me there. I had to change and make tough sacrifices. It was tough but I needed to walk my road alone for a little while. It was the first obstacle that I had to overcome but it wouldn't be the last.

I marched on through school and eventually found myself having completed the entire EMT program. This was such a great accomplishment in my eyes. It was something I was, and still am, very proud of. I didn't allow myself to get too distracted, though. I knew that there was still a long road ahead so I kept my focus and moved forward.

By this time, I had moved on from construction but still found myself apart of the manual labor work force. I was now working for Lowe's Distributing Center in Mount Vernon. It was much closer to my classes, in Mount Pleasant. At the distribution center, I would load and unload eighteen-wheelers. Lowe's carries a million different products. I'd bet you that I loaded at least one of everything in those trucks. It was different work but the same ole grind.

Summers in Texas are notoriously hot and the heat was exceptionally brutal that summer. I sweated like crazy as I loaded and unloaded those trucks. I must've lost thirty pounds that summer. This was well before my bodybuilding days. I was still just a tall, scrawny kid. I didn't have thirty pounds to lose. This was another job that further pushed me to get my education and move on with my career.

When I managed to get time off from Lowe's, I worked as an on-call EMT in Clarksville, just a few miles down the road. Not too long into my Clarksville gig, Life-Net offered me a full time job as an EMT in Texarkana. I was ecstatic. I could finally ditch the manual labor industry and work at something I was truly passionate about. This was the first time in my life that I had worked toward and accomplished something I really wanted. My hard work was paying off. I would grow addicted to this feeling of accomplishment and fulfillment.

The schedule was great. I'd work twenty-four hours on and have forty-eight hours off. Now, it's not twenty-four hours of non-stop work. As an EMT, paramedic, or even a firefighter, you have plenty of downtime. This time is either spent at the station cleaning or resting, or riding around in the ambulance. This schedule allowed me to get extra studying in during our downtime.

We had a great crew there in Texarkana. My partner, Joe Fritz, was quite the character. I enjoyed working with Joe very much. He was ex-military and one fine paramedic. I consider myself very fortunate to work by his side. He knew everything there was to know about the human body. He could tell you how the body responded to trauma and various types of medicine. You name it and Joe knew it. I learned a lot from my hands on experience with Joe.

Everywhere Joe went he carried a guitar with him. Even in the ambulance, he'd bring it along and crank out a few tunes when we weren't busy. When Joe wasn't at work, he played in a blues band called "Code Blue." I found that to be very clever seeing that our paramedic uniforms were blue and that he played the blues. The whole thing was pretty cool. Joe knew just about every Buddy Guy and Stevie Ray Vaughn song there was. This job had turned out to be the most enjoyable work experiences I ever had. My motivation was at an all time high. I was excited about where my career was going.

Paramedic school would turn out to be a bit more extensive than I had anticipated. Looking back, it's clear to see why that is. As a paramedic, you never know what you're going to be required to do when you arrive at a call. We had to learn about pharmacology (uses, effects, and modes of action of drugs), emergency medicine, advanced airway techniques… The list went on and on. Therefore, the curriculum attempts to cover everything.

It was like a crash course to become a doctor. In fact, once you become certified as a paramedic, there's not much more that doctor's can do than you. The program was incredibly extensive and fast-paced with a seventy-five percent failure rate. Only one out of every four would pass this class. The last thing I wanted to do was get behind.

I worked relentlessly to stay ahead. Ultimately, I made it through the program. Not only did I finish, I somehow managed to graduate at the top of my class. I passed the extensive two-day test the very first time, which is not a common accomplishment. That's right, the guy who was in special education courses in high school graduated top of his paramedic class. It just goes to show you that if you want anything bad enough, nothing can stop you.

I had completed the most difficult part of the program but still had a very long ways to go. I needed to complete 1,300 hours of clinical rotations. I completed these on the weekends, without pay. I spent countless hours in the emergency room (ER), operating room (OR), labor delivery and the ambulance. I was still working as an EMT but I wasn't allowed to count those toward my clinical hours.

Although I had zero time for anything else, this was a very proud time in my life. I was beginning to get a sense of who I was and what this life required of me. I was improving each and every day, which I have found to be a big key for individual happiness. I was making a difference and leaving each workday with a great sense of fulfillment.

I believe that finding something that fulfills is a very rare thing these days. It saddens me that most people aren't happy in their current jobs. I wasn't happy when I was working construction or loading trucks. I wasn't in a position to grow. I didn't feel like my work was making a difference. Regardless of whether your work is making a difference or not, what really matters is if you feel like you're making a difference. I think it's imperative for those in similar situations to find a way out. Get a plan together and start making some moves. Nothing is going to change unless you act. If you truly want to be happy, you need to be in the right environment to grow and achieve that sense of fulfillment. What work do you truly want to do? Don't tell me that you can't afford to do it. The truth is: you can't afford not to.

Take some time to think about what would make you excited to wake up each day. Don't be foolish about it. Not every day is going to be great. You'll have bad days but the good ones will make up the difference. In the long run, you'll see the fruits of your labor. When that begins to happen, it's a beautiful thing my friend. Enjoy it and use it to fuel your drive to achieving your heart's desire.

I was sure happy to have conquered this difficult part of the process. It challenged me and I grew stronger from facing the challenge and overcoming it. I was becoming stronger and more confident with each passing day. I capitalized on this momentum and took it with me, as I faced my future obstacles. There was more work to be done. I was just getting started.

CHAPTER THREE

"Life as a Paramedic"

"My dad shot me."

Those were the final words of a young boy, whom I watch die, in my arms. His father had gone crazy, shooting the boy and his mother. When we arrived at the scene, we found the boy in the driveway, clinging to life with each breath. Holding the boy in my arms, I knew very well the fate of this kid. It saddened me to no end that there would be little I could do to help. Things like that still bother me. This kid's whole life was in front of him. It was now being stripped away before it ever really began. That's one call I'll never forget, as long as I live.

I took great pride in being a paramedic. To this day, I consider it my greatest accomplishment. I had learned everything I could during school. My goal was to be as prepared as best I could for real-life situations. I completely gave up drinking and partying. I believed my patients deserved to have me at my absolute best. But, all of the studying, exams, and practical's couldn't prepare you for everything that you'd face in the line of duty.

The life of a paramedic is a rollercoaster. It's just the nature of the job. One call you could save a life, the very next you could watch someone take his or her last breath. Despite your best efforts, sometimes there's just nothing you can do. It was frustrating at times when circumstances were beyond intervention. As a medic, or even a doctor, there is only so much that you can do.

As paramedics or EMTs, we were never taught to diagnose. Our job was to treat the symptoms, which you practically had to diagnose the problem, in order to treat the symptoms appropriately. More often than not, I was dealing with either medical issues or trauma. Medical calls involved patients having something going wrong inside of them, such as a heart attack. Trauma would be someone suffering from a broken limb or head injury.

Our actions upon arriving at the scene could be very impactful on the patient's situation. However, the majority of the care would come from the hospital. As a paramedic, out in the real world, we were very limited with what we could do. The best thing for us would be to address and help what we could then get the patient to the nearest appropriate hospital. If that meant I had to call in a helicopter to get them there, that's what I did. I say nearest appropriate hospital because not every hospital has the requirements to meet the patient's needs. If the patient is in a critical condition, their best chances for survival are within the first hour. This is often referred to as the Golden Hour.

After numerous calls, I eventually developed this sixth sense. On the way to the call, I'd be going over different circumstances that we could face upon arrival. I'd see myself following the proper procedure and helping the patient as best I could. When I arrived to the call, I addressed the situation and did what needed to be done. After doing so, I had a feeling that I knew what the outcome would be. I developed a pretty good knack for knowing what was going on with them and the likelihood of their fate. I didn't always find this ability a good thing. It was tough to deal with that information. The feeling of knowing that there was nothing else I could do never sat well with me.

It was difficult to deal with, at times. I tried to remain mindful that God was in control. I was put in circumstances as a medium for God to work through me. Although it wasn't easy, I tried not to take the outcomes personal. I did everything I could to make sure that I'd be ready for every call. While at the scene, I did everything I could, as best I could. When it wasn't enough, it certainly hurt but there wasn't much else I could do. I had to accept the situation as it was.

I have numerous events that will be forever imprinted in my mind. Some days life as a paramedic was just rough. I've seen people need to be cut from a car, bodies scattered on the highway, people shot, and more than I'd like to remember. Those kinds of days were pretty rough but it's what I signed up for. Every time you get a call you're heading to help somebody in a situation that nobody would want to be in. I was prepared, as best you could be, for it. In this line of work, lives are at stake. It's different from business where a bad day could be losing money or having to fire somebody. A bad day here usually means that a life was lost. A family loses their father or mother, brother or sister.

As sad as it is to say, you get use to the grotesque; it becomes normal. Heck, we'd go work a call where people needed to be airlifted to the hospital, after a two car accident, blood all over the road, people screaming in pain. We showed up, did what we could do, and then carry on with lunch half an hour later, as if nothing abnormal had happened.

Some days were difficult but there were good days too. As low as the bad days were, the good days were even better. The good days made everything worth it. This one fall afternoon, we received a call from a doctor's office in Bogota, TX. Bogota is an incredibly small town, probably best described as a community. The nearest hospital is twenty minutes away. It took us over half an hour to arrive on the scene.

We arrive and as I walk through the door, I immediately begin making an assessment, as per protocol. I see a man on the floor and he seems to be semi-conscious. I attempt to communicate with him and he's barely able to respond. I check his pulse; it's crazy fast. I throw a heart monitor and an oxygen mask on him. I quickly realize that he is in supra ventricular tachycardia (SVT). The upper chambers of his heart were opening and closing too fast and were not filling up properly. This wasn't good.

My initial protocol yielded no results, so I moved on to the next step. I hit him with the defibrillator panels. When you do this, there's always a chance you can completely stop the heart. The goal with the defibrillator is to shock the heart back into a normal rhythm but there's always that chance of it not working according to plan.

I rub the paddles together to spread the gel placed on them. (That's not just something you see in movies.) I push the paddles down on his chest and see his eyes roll back in his head. "Shit, I just killed this guy," I thought. I look over to the heart monitor and the guy is now pulseless. His heart is quivering inside his chest. I quickly readjust the settings on the defibrillator and hit him with the paddles once more. He flops on the floor and comes back to life. He opened his eyes and looked directly up at me. I vividly remember the next thing that happened. I'll never forget it. The guy looked up at me and said, "damn, my chest hurts!"

We exchanged a brief smile and then smoothly, but quickly, got him in the ambulance and carried him to the hospital. The guy talked to me the entire ride there. Turned out, he had a history of heart problems. I later found out that he lived another nine years after that incident. Heck, I think he was about eighty years old that day.

As a paramedic, it's rare to see or learn about the long-term outcomes of your intervention. Typically, once you get the patient to where they need to be, that's the last you hear. Unless, you happen to read about it in the paper or decide to follow up. In my early days of being a paramedic, I would sometimes do a little research to find out how the patient was doing. That didn't last long, as I just couldn't handle the bad news. You either love being a paramedic or you hate it.

There's really no gray area in between. I loved what I did and I was good at. I never had so much fulfillment in all my life.

* * * * * * *

I've never been able to fully let go of that part of my life. I loved being a paramedic. I loved helping people in desperate need. I loved going into work each day. It's tough to give up things you love and care about. I've done numerous things to help fill the void but none of them have completely taken the place of being a paramedic. While it's unfortunate that I can no longer work as a paramedic, it wouldn't do me much good to sit around and cry about it. I've got to carry on and continue to live the best life that I can. That's pretty much the only option that I have. My situation is what it is and I have to live with that. I refuse to throw in the towel just because a few things didn't go my way.

I believe everything happens for a reason and what doesn't kill you makes you stronger. It's cliché to say but it is true. What doesn't kill you can make you stronger, if you allow it to do so. Initially, you'll feel bitter but if you continue to feel bitter about the situation instead of trying to make the most of it, you're in for a long, rough road. If I've learned anything over the last few decades, it's that the obstacles that appear to be in your way actually start to become the way. Those barriers will create opportunities you never would've considered.

When your back is against the wall and you're given no other choice but to be strong and fight back, you may just surprise yourself on what you are truly capable of. Don't underestimate yourself, never think that all is lost and always make the best your situation. Carry yourself with a little grit and swagger. Walk with confidence and live up to your potential.

Answering The Call

CHAPTER FOUR

"Building the Body"

After working for Life-Net from 1997-2000, I was hired by Red River Army Depot (RRAD). There I would work as a paramedic and firefighter. My long-term goal was to be a flight medic, on a helicopter. In order to accomplish that task, I would need a few more years of experience. I figured once I got more experience, I could pursue that goal more seriously. The job at Red River was another confirmation that I was on the right path and doing great work.

"So… you're telling me, that you guys are going pay me… to go to the gym?" I asked.

"Well, yeah. You're a firefighter. You've gotta stay in shape." They responded.

I was pretty excited after having that conversation. I was already plenty pumped up after being offered the position. This was just icing on the cake. I was making good money. I had a great work schedule. I would be able to afford a gym membership, and possibly even some of those high dollar supplements that could help me pack on some muscle. Now was the time to get serious about this whole bodybuilding thing.

When I was a kid, I was a bit chunky. As I matured and grew taller, I didn't gain much weight, which left me tall and lanky with little muscle mass. I remember my grandfather saying, "You ain't nothin' but skin and bones, boy!" I was always intrigued with the physiques of Super Man and Rocky. I thought there bodies were solid displays of masculinity. I wanted to be just like them. I did push ups and sit ups at the house and broke many household items trying to duplicate scenes from their movies.

My first attempt with bodybuilding came when I started working for Life-Net, in Texarkana. I stumbled upon an old Muscle Media Magazine. Inside it had several people who had gone through incredible twelve-week transformations. These men and women went from obese to shredded, literally. Knowing what I know now about the fitness industry, I'm sure that these photos had some digital enhancements done to them. Much of the same goes on today, I'm sorry to say. And, just like many people today, I was fooled. The advertisement was highlighting the benefits of their new protein bar. I was sold that it would help me pack on some muscle. So, in 2000, I bought my first supplement: the Myoplex Protein Bar. It wasn't bad but by today's standards would almost be uneatable.

I found an old gym in downtown Texarkana called Law Dogs. It served primarily law enforcement and service providers, such as EMTs. It reminded me of an old Metroflex Gym. It was dirty and very old school with the bare minimum equipment. It had the kind of vibe that would attract serious lifters.

I somehow convinced a buddy of mine to join me for my first workout. We decided that we would train legs and boy did we do 'em. After completing about fifty working sets of squats, leg extensions, hamstring curls, leg press, and lunges, we stumbled out of the gym not knowing what the next few days would bring. Twenty-four hours later, I could hardly walk. Getting in and out of the ambulance had become a very difficult task. My buddy was so sore that had to call in sick to work. Some serious doubts filled my head; I wasn't quite sure this whole bodybuilding thing was for me. I wasn't committed and pretty much stopped working out after that. Fast forward a few years, I was hired by Red River and would have an hour every day to workout. I didn't know much more about bodybuilding than the first time I attempted it; but, I decided to give it another shot.

During my first year of training, I saw very little progress. I knew very little about workout routines and even less about the nutritional aspect. I picked up things here and there from various lifters that I had met in the gym. I started to get a real hunger for information, much like during EMT school. I began searching for materials to read and learn from. I picked up a copy of Arnold Schwarzenegger's *Encyclopedia on Bodybuilding*. I figured if anybody knew anything about bodybuilding it would be the eight time Mr. Olympia.

It was like being back in paramedic school. I read everything I could get my hands on. I was staying up late reading and structuring my workouts on paper. Once again, I had found something that sparked a fire inside of me. I began force-feeding myself six meals a day until it became routine. I had programmed workouts that were specific to me and my goals of building muscle. I deployed a ton of patience, although there were many times where my patience wore thin. Three years later, I was standing at a solid 240 pounds and about fifteen percent body fat.

Around this time, I was beginning to get a lot of pressure from friends and lifting partners to compete in a bodybuilding show. I was always inspired by bodybuilders who competed but never did I consider doing a show myself. I didn't get into bodybuilding to compete. I just wanted to put on some size and get stronger, maybe even look a little better in a T-shirt.

In 2003, I was finally convinced to do a show. With the help of a good friend and mentor, Jeff Johnson, I decided to compete in the oldest running show in the state, The Heart of Texas. Jeff was a few years younger than I was but he was very knowledgeable in the sport. He had won the Arkansas State Championship and provided me invaluable insight over the last few years. He structured my diet and workouts in great detail. I trusted Jeff and he did not disappoint.

Getting ready for a bodybuilding show required me to change a few things with my training and diet. The preparation was hard but like most bodybuilders, I enjoyed the struggle. The structure and discipline it required of me was what I appreciated the most. I certainly didn't do it for the attention or money. There is absolutely zero money to be made in amateur bodybuilding. In fact, it costs you quite a bit of money. Add up the entry fees, tanning, travel and lodging costs, not to mention the food and supplements. You could go on a short vacation with the money you spend to compete in a bodybuilding show.

Even at the highest of levels of bodybuilding, the small fortunes are nothing compared to other professional sports. The Mr. Olympia is the Super Bowl of bodybuilding. Since it's creation in 1965, by Joe Weider, there have only been thirteen men to claim the title. The winner receives one million dollars. While one million dollars is a large sum of money, in the context of other sports, it's pennies in comparison. Bodybuilders must get sponsorships in order to compete. Many athletes compete on their own dime.

The sport of bodybuilding is very misunderstood. Some see bodybuilders as egotistical and selfish. I'll agree that it's difficult to keep your eyes from rolling when you see somebody flexing in the mirror. It's just part of the sport. Posing is a very crucial component. Men and women flex to see where they may need to make improvements. I think Arnold described it best. Bodybuilders are like sculptors. A sculptor looks at his work and decides that it's not as proportionate as it should be. The sculptor then adds more clay and begins to even things out. Bodybuilders do the same thing. It just takes longer and requires more struggle.

In my experience, I have met some of the most humble, caring, and respectful people in the sport of bodybuilding. I'm not saying that there aren't assholes out there. Every profession has its share of people who give the rest a bad name. But, I have learned that those people are few and far between. You don't get too far, in bodybuilding or life, by being disrespectful or selfish. Nobody can deny a bodybuilder's hard work. It's on display for all to see but bodybuilding is about much more than just what you look like.

For me, bodybuilding sums up dedication and discipline. It gives me structure and a sense of purpose. It keeps my mind focused and prevents me from having too much idle time on my hands. I'm not sure where I'd be without bodybuilding. It's not just about muscle. Being strong in the gym is truly secondary. The strength I develop in the gym transitions into inner strength. The journey and the process is what I truly love. Competing just gives me something to look forward to and keeps me on track.

I wish not to force-feed anybody with bodybuilding. It makes me happy but something else may make you happy. Everybody has something that they need to do in order to achieve their desired happiness. It's extremely rare that people find this happiness with their jobs or daily routine. Therefore, it's imperative that they find an avenue to express their passions and gifts. I consider myself extremely blessed to have found work and hobbies that I am truly passionate about.

The hard work in the gym, the discipline required with food and calories, and the necessary time to rest and recover from workouts provides one with the utmost structure. It has always kept me focused and consistent. That's what I truly love about bodybuilding. If it had been all about winning trophies and getting paid, I would've quit a long time ago, probably after my first show.

I remember showing up to check-ins on that Friday night. I was served the biggest piece of humble pie ever. "Are we in the right place?" I asked my buddy. "All these guys look like they pull up tree stumps for a living." I was in a room full of monsters. Everybody was huge. My confidence took quite the hit that night. But, I had put in all the hard work and stayed disciplined. I was already there, might as well see how I measured up. I had chiseled down to 190 pounds. I estimated my body fat to be around eight percent or so. Not bad, I thought, having started at 240 pounds and fifteen percent body fat.

I was one of the smallest guys in my heavy weight class but I managed to earn ninth place out of fifteen competitors. It was hardly something to brag about but I was proud of the accomplishment. I had never done anything like this before. I wasn't the most excited about being on stage in front of a crowd, with all eyes on me. Overcoming that fear should be considered a win for anybody! I set a goal, worked hard to achieve it, and I was proud of what I did and presented it on stage.

After my show, I realized that my genetic potential for bodybuilding didn't align with my enthusiasm. My bodybuilding expectations became a lot more realistic. I still loved the sport and planned on continuing the lifestyle but any thoughts I had of becoming a professional bodybuilder quickly vanished. I still loved the sport but stepping back on stage wasn't something I had in my immediate plans. In fact, the 2003 Heart of Texas would be the first and only time I would step on stage as an able-body competitor.

Despite the average finish, my confidence in life was soaring at an all time high. I had a job that I loved and was excelling at. I was proud of what I did to transform my body, through discipline and hard work. That confidence began spilling into every other aspect of life. There was nothing I couldn't do and I made it my mission to get the most out of this one shot at life!

Answering The Call

CHAPTER FIVE

"Flying High"

    I felt on top of the world. I wish I could bottle this feeling up and give it to people. If people only knew how powerful that sense of accomplishment truly was. They would stop sitting around making excuses as to why they haven't done what they know they should. They'd take on each day with a newly found enthusiasm. Everything I was setting my sites on I was accomplishing. The past few years of hard work, dedication, and sweat equity had all paid off, exponentially. My career was going better than I ever could've imagined. I was newly married. I had transformed my physical body into something I had long desired. In doing so, I was gifted with a self-confidence and mental fortitude that convinced me that I was capable of anything.

After the Heart of Texas bodybuilding show, my confidence continued to soar. It was almost as if, I had won the entire show. I didn't bring home any trophies. I brought back something even better, something I could carry with me and use in every endeavor moving forward: a soaring confidence that nobody could bring down. I had gone from a kid who knew absolutely nothing about what he wanted to do with his life, to a man who was fulfilling his purpose and doing some pretty cool stuff along the way.

I had turned my sites to the field of aviation. As a kid, I was amazed at how airplanes could fly. To this day, I still have quite the astonishment for how air travel has made the world a much smaller place. We now have access to some of the most remote places on earth. I didn't learn to fly so that I could go all over the world, necessarily. I just wanted to experience that thrill and do something few others will.

The first airplane I remember seeing was a crop duster. Those pilots were crazy. You could (and still can) see them along Interstate 30 traveling through Arkansas. They would give the interstate traffic quite a show and sometimes a nice little scare. They would dive down and look as though they were about to crash into oncoming traffic. They would pull up at the very last moment, leaving the drivers heart racing, I'm sure. I never intended to do such stunts. I just wished to fly and soar among the clouds and view the world from a different perspective.

My ultimate goal with being a paramedic was to eventually become a flight medic. So, learning to fly wasn't all just fun and games. It had real world application for me. I was a few years of experience and training away from becoming a flight medic. My plan was to work at Red River and get the experience I needed and then change up career paths to eventually become a flight medic.

In the fall of 2004, not long after my first bodybuilding show, I started learning to fly. A friend of mine informed me about the Texarkana Flying School. One day I decided to go scope it out and see what they had to offer. A buddy came with me to the airport and we were able to meet with the instructor. We sparked a conversation that eventually led to him offering to take us for a ride in the plane, to see if we liked it. My buddy wasn't too keen on the idea but I jumped at the offer, like a kid at Christmas. One flight was all it took; I was hooked.

The biggest barrier to entry, at least initially, was the cost. Flying isn't necessarily a cheap hobby. Each time you had to pay for the instructor, the gas, and the time using the plane. The study materials and testing weren't free either. I talked it over with my (then) wife and she was all for it. We didn't have any kids and were making decent money between the two of us. It didn't put us in a bind financially.

Compared to paramedic school, learning to fly was a breeze. The difficulty was finding the time to do it. Twice a week I would drive out to Texarkana Regional Airport. It would cost me several hours of my time. Twenty minutes to get there, half an hour to ready the plane, fly for an hour or so, land the plane and tidy up the hanger. All in all, it was about a three or four hour process.

Was it worth it? Hell yeah, it was worth it. Flying gives you a sense of rare freedom. It's almost a completely different world up there. Heck, flying even has it's own language and time. Each time I was up in the air it was an awesome experience. Soaring over the piney woods of Northeast Texas is an experience I'll never forget. And, although I wasn't completely alone, I always found a breath of freedom *flying high*.

In order to fly solo, you must pass all the educational requirements and log sixteen to twenty hours of flight time with an instructor. Each time I sat in the plane I gained more and more confidence but it's a whole different game when you're in the plane alone. It's quite intimidating to even think about it. I remember my first time flying solo. I showed up to fly one afternoon, knowing that my hours were getting close to fulfilling the requirements. But, we readied the plane and I went up with the instructor. A small sense of relief filled me, as I had anticipated that he would say today was the day I'd fly solo.

We flew and when it came time to head back to the airport the instructor told me to land the plane but not to shut off the engine. When he told me that, I knew that I was about to fly solo for the very first time. My heart began to race and continued to increase as I set the plane down, taxied over to the hanger, and brought the plane to a stop. The instructor opened his door and hopped out. He looked back at me and yelled over the engine's roar, "you ready?!"

"Do you think I'm ready?" I yelled back.

"Wouldn't be getting out if I didn't think you were!" he said, as he slammed the door.

My sites quickly turned from the instructor to all of the switches and gauges of the plane. For a brief instance, all the knowledge I had about how to operate this plane evaded me.

I might as well been staring at the human brain. Luckily, that panic and fear quickly subsided and my instincts and habits took over. I taxied back over to the runway and slowly put the throttle down. The power of 130 horses was unleashed and before I knew it, I was speeding down the runway and took off in the air.

That feeling of flying is something that I can't even begin to describe. To this day, I think about those moments, being so high above the earth and seeing things from a new perspective. It's one of the few activities I have found that completely allows you to escape. You forget everything that's not going on directly in front of you. I really appreciated that about flying. I think, as humans, we crave those types of healthy escapes. But, more often than not, we allow fear to get in the way of experiencing them.

It's difficult to find places to escape the routine of daily life. I've found it necessary to do so, though. It keeps things interesting and allows you view daily life in a new light upon your return. It keeps things interesting and fun. I was proud of myself for putting myself through this challenge and growing from the experience. Flying was another thing I could rest my hat on and say that I did.

Maybe I was addicted to the feeling of accomplishment. Setting out to do something and working hard to succeed was incredibly rewarding. The human being is far too often underrated and underappreciated. We are capable of some pretty cool things. We are able to achieve whatever we set our minds to. Through each success I witnessed my confidence grow stronger. What could I not do? I began to set my sites on the next adventure, all the while keeping up with my job, bodybuilding, my marriage, and flying.

Senior Prom with step brother, Chad Whitecotton (1992)

My grandfather, James Butler McCrary

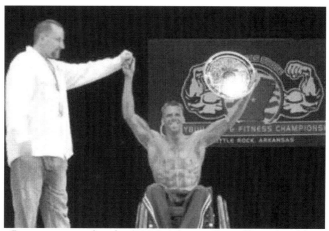

Best poser award at the (2007) Arkansas State Championships

[Left] One of the few pictures I have as an able body competitor (2003)

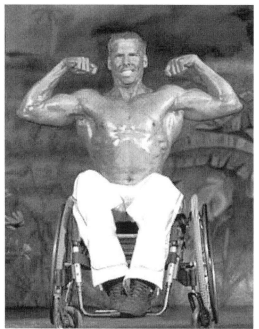
First bodybuilding show in a wheelchair (2005)

An article from the Texarkana Gazette a few weeks before stepping back on stage, only 6 months after injury

Flexing after a workout with friend and training partner, Jon Minter

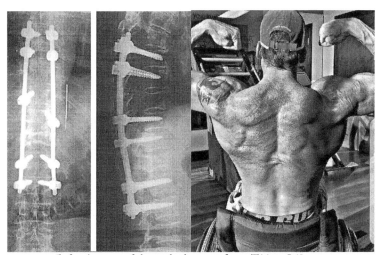

[left: pictures of the rods that run from T11 to L1]

While working construction and driving "Old Blue," I told myself that I'd drive a better car one day. This is my current ride.

Just a few of the many trophies I've earned during my bodybuilding career with Super Man overlooking.

A rare picture of me wearing shorts. You can see the atrophy of my legs compared to my upper body.

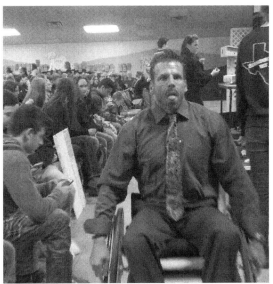

Having some fun before speaking at a local high school

Here I am as a young child with my mom.

Super Man has always been a figure in my life

National Wheelchair Championships (2016)

National Wheelchair Championships (2017)

Speaking at an FFA event in Lindale, TX.
800+ Students, largest speaking to date.

Insert Text Here...

First brochure that I made to answer the call to start speaking

National Stage in 2008. I took home first in Heavyweight and and Masters Would take second in the overall and miss earning my pro card by one placing

Chad McCrary

Answering The Call

CHAPTER SIX

"Clouds & Dirt"

It may seem like I had a bucket list of items I wanted to do as a kid and that I was casually checking them off one by one. There wasn't a list, per say. I was a very ambitious person. In many regards, I still very much am. I was a yes man, saying yes to things that excited me and gave me an opportunity to do something I have never done before. It seemed as if I had life by the tail. Many of my childhood dreams had developed into realities. I had always lived for the thrill of an adrenaline rush. I soon turned my sites to my next challenge.

Many of these adventures were rooted back to my childhood. Being a small town kid, I wasn't able to do a whole lot while growing up. When opportunities arose, as an adult, I wouldn't dare allow them to pass. Some may say that I never grew up. Whatever that means. I believe that we all have that little kid still inside of us. We become depressed and ungrateful when our child-like wonder escapes us.

Seeing pictures of Evil Knievel soaring through the air on a motorcycle over a dozen junkyard cars impressed the heck out of my younger self. My intentions with a dirt bike were never to that extreme but things like that certainly made me think it'd be cool to have a bike. I remember a kid in my neighborhood had a black and yellow, two-stroke Yamaha. We weren't necessarily friends. He was a bit of a troublemaker. He always had cuts and bruises on his arms and legs from dirt bike accidents. That was precisely why I never had a bike growing up. There was no way my parents were going to allow that; they didn't have the money to afford one anyway. Regardless, I wanted to ride and I was set on making that happen sooner or later.

It's no big secret that dirt bikes and motorcycles are inherently dangerous; that's just their nature. I knew this then. I certainly know it now. But, I was never one to live out of fear. In fact, I did my best to face fear dead in the eye with a smile on my face. Living in a fearful state is no way to live. You can find danger everywhere if you're looking for it. You can also find joy and good wherever you look. It's all about your perception.

The same fall that I learned to fly; I would also learn to ride. In the fall of 2004, a few of my close friends began to ride motocross. One night, I went to the track with them and watched them ride. It didn't take long for me to decide that I didn't want to just watch. My time of sitting on the sidelines was over. I wanted to be in on the action.

The very next day, I found myself in the Yamaha store buying the biggest, baddest bike they had. This was during the time when two-strokes were beginning to fade out in order to make way for the more popular four-strokes. The sound and smell of my childhood neighbor's two-stroke was embedded in my head. I was dead set on a two-stroke and signed a check for a brand new YZ250. You could say that it was my unyielding appetite for an adrenaline rush that prompted this purchase. I just couldn't sit back and watch.

I've always found myself to be a quick learner and learning to ride was no exception. I caught on very quickly and found myself doing sixty-foot doubles in no time. We had a small, tight-knit group that would visit all the local tracks. One weekend we would be in Hooks, TX. The next weekend we would be headed down to Shreveport, LA. We had a blast riding together and the adrenaline we all got from riding and hitting jumps was addicting. We couldn't get enough. I was experiencing new speeds among the clouds and now in the dirt.

We weren't blind to the dangers of riding bikes. There had been several crashes at the tracks that we had witnessed. We saw people miss jumps, land awkwardly, and turn bikes over. We knew that there was real danger involved. We were well aware of the dangers involved but never really talked about it. We didn't need to. It wouldn't do us any good to dwell on that. Everybody knows that there's a risk of injury every time you strap up the boots but you don't go around talking about it every day. I've heard riding motorcycles put like this before: the longer you ride, the more likely you are to go down. You just hope that you survive when you do.

We rode all fall, right up until Thanksgiving. During the holidays, we all got busy and just didn't have time to get out to the tracks. The conditions weren't the most favorable during these months, as the tracks saw quite a bit of rain. Believe it or not, riding is a bit more enjoyable in the cooler weather. During the summer, the bike gets incredibly hot. Combine that with the infamous Texas heat and it doesn't make for the most enjoyable riding experience.

February came around and I was itching to get back on the track. I would even crank my bike in the garage and let it run. I couldn't get enough of the sound of the motor and the smell of the exhaust. It wouldn't be long before I'd have her back on the track.

The first weekend in March we were back on the track. We bounced from track to track because each one had something different to offer. Whichever one we felt like riding that day, is the one we'd go to. The track in Hooks was an intermediate one, for a bit more experienced riders. I had caught on very quickly the previous fall and had worked my way up to seventy-five foot doubles. My confidence grew upon each successful landing. I should note that I wasn't completely reckless on my bike. None of us were. The track in Hooks had a 120-foot jump that I didn't dare try. Each jump, though risky, was calculated and planned. I did my best to prepare before attempting each jump.

A few weekends later, we decided to ride the track in Plain Dealings, LA. I had never ridden this track before so I was excited to see what this track had to offer. This track gave you the opportunity to hit a triple, about 100 feet long, if you dared. We road for several hours. I had consistently single-doubled this jump, meaning that I would hit the first jump and land on the very next side then hit the gas and ramp off the next mound and land on the other side of the adjacent mound. My buddies had been tripling this jump and were giving me shit about single doubling. I wasn't yet comfortable enough to try the triple.

Four-wheelers, or quads, were allowed on this track. They're notorious for rutting up the runs, especially around the berms. This 100-foot jump came right out of a berm or corner turn. I had trouble getting enough traction coming out of this turn, due to the ruts made from the four-wheelers. I found it tough to double it, much less triple. I decided to play it safe and single the first and double the second.

As things were winding down for the day, I gave the jump some serious thought. My confidence had grown on this new track. I eventually convinced myself that I would give this triple a shot. I told my buddies that I was about to triple that jump. "You're a chicken shit if you don't!" they encouraged me. I wouldn't say that it was peer pressure that convinced me to do it. I decided on my own terms. I thought I could make it. I took a few more laps and mentally prepared for the attempt. I was getting to know my bike better and better with each lap. Sometimes two-strokes can be a bit wiry and unpredictable. It takes a good amount of time to get use to it and know what to expect from it, in different situations.

I turned the corner to start a new lap and was committed to giving this triple a shot. I came into the berm, hoping to get more traction than previous runs. I did. I made it to third gear and hit the throttle hard. I launched into the air. Everything was so good so far. I immediately began accessing the situation, in mid-air. I looked down and saw the middle jump passing under the bike. Everything was still good. I looked forward to scope out the landing. My heart sank. Judging by my trajectory, I was going to come up short.

This mound wasn't the most forgiving. To land safely, I would need to clear the mound's peak and land on the down slope. There wasn't much room for error. Thoughts raced through my head. Should I jump off the bike or ride it out? The bike had good suspension. Maybe I should just ride it out. If I jumped off, how would I land? All these thoughts flashed in my head in a matter of seconds. I decided that I would trust the suspension and stay on the bike.

The bike landed on its motor casing. The suspension was never able to relieve any of the impact. I slammed into the seat and all the energy transferred through the bike into my back and up through my spinal cord. I experienced a big flash of lighting, like fireworks exploding right in front of my face. The bike went onto its front tire and flipped with me still on it. Eventually, my momentum stopped and the bike and I would come to a halt, the bike resting on top of me, still running.

At this point, I couldn't feel much of anything. I never lost consciousness and felt no pain, at this point. The world was dark. I was face down. I felt the bike pulled off of me. My heart beating heavily inside of my chest. I felt weird, like my legs had been ripped from my body. It was as if I only existed from the waist up. I heard people talking all around me, with panic in their voices.

"Don't touch him." one voice yelled.

"Somebody call an ambulance!" another voice yelled.

Then I heard a familiar voice. "Chad, get up man." I attempted to push myself up from the dirt but my legs didn't move. I lay back down after this failed attempt. "Come on dude, get up! Chad! Get up!" my buddy yelled with fear in his voice.

Thoughts filled my head. I was pretty sure that I had broken my back, based on the neurological feedback (big flash I had seen earlier). The lack of response and feeling from my lower body was also a very telling sign. My career, my marriage, my entire life all flashed before me. Is this it? Is it all over? I found myself in a completely new reality, a very messed up one.

In the distance, I could hear a helicopter. Each passing moment it got closer and closer. The sound of the blades chopping through the air grew louder and louder. I knew that was my ride out of here. What seemed like an eternity, took only fifteen minutes. They put me on a spine board with a C collar around my neck. Being a paramedic, I knew that this was standard protocol. I remained optimistic even though I was almost sure my back was broken. Things weren't looking good.

They took me to LSU medical hospital in Shreveport. Once in the helicopter, I recalled seeing a lonely pair of boots in the dirt. I looked down and found that my boots had been taken off. I never felt them being removed. Around that time, I started experiencing a tremendous amount of pain. The pain grew stronger by the second. I told the flight medic to give me something for the pain. He said that he couldn't. My patience expired as the pain grew to unbearable levels.

"Give me some damn Morphine, Demoral, Nubane, Tordall! Give me something man! I know you've got it!" I said impatiently. The flight medic responded inquisitively, "How do you know that?" I pointed to his sleeve and told him that I was a nationally certified paramedic just like him. It was only a fifteen-minute flight. He didn't want to give me anything if he didn't have to. I insisted that he did and he gave me some morphine but it didn't even put a dent in the pain. This would be just the beginning of months of relentless pain. I had no idea what was to come.

When I arrived at LSU, they immediately ran tests, which would confirm my suspicions. Lying in a hospital bed, hearing the news that I had broken my back and would likely never walk again was a nightmare, a living nightmare. Although I had clearly heard what the doctor said, I asked him to repeat himself, hoping that somehow I had misunderstood what he said. No such luck.

I had major swelling and blood clots in my back. I would have to wait for the swelling to go down before they could operate. I would wait a week before surgery. During the ten-hour surgery, doctors would pick out 142 pieces of my T12 vertebra. It had virtually exploded inside my body. My spinal cord had been about ninety percent severed. They were worried about stabilizing my back so they needed to put rods on both sides of my spine. Those rods run from my T11 down to L1 (mid back). Those rods are still in my back today and will likely remain there forever.

After taking post surgery x-rays, the doctor once again told me that it was highly unlikely that I'd ever walk again. "I've seen this kind of injury a bunch." He said. "It's very likely that you'll never be able to walk again." That really stung. I've been called a lot of things but "like most people" has never been one of them. I remained optimistic that I would be okay and maybe, just maybe, would one day walk again.

Just as I thought that things couldn't get much worse, I was going through some mail and ran across an envelope from the National Registry of EMTs. The letter would inform me that I had completed all the requirements and I was officially recognized as a Nationally Certified Paramedic. The envelope included a patch that would be sown on to my uniform. I would never wear that patch in the line of duty. In this moments, I was reminded that my future was about to drastically change. I had tried to remained optimistic throughout everything that I had just gone through but this was a hit that I could've done without.

Answering The Call

CHAPTER SEVEN

"Plan the Flight. Fly the Plan."

I had spent too much time in Shreveport. I wanted to be back in Texarkana, near home. I thought things would be a little more normal there or at least a bit more familiar. The doctors recommended that I stay. It would be a complicated ride back to Texas. I didn't really like that answer so I took it upon myself to make a few calls. My previous unit at Life-Net would send an ambulance to transfer me back to Bowie County. It was the longest hour and half ride of my entire life. Ambulances aren't known for their smooth ride. I felt every bump and a tremendous amount of pain. I begged the question, "when would this pain subside?"

I arrived at St. Michael Rehab Center in April of 2005. I would spend over ninety days there. I even celebrated my birthday from the hospital room. I lost a ton of weight due to the lack of appetite. Two weeks passed before I ate anything substantial. I wasn't hungry and no food seemed to taste good.

I had gone from soaring through the clouds to crashing hard, in the dirt. My confidence and sense of purpose seemed to crash with me. My future was uncertain but I had many people on my side. I was surrounded by top-notch therapists who encouraged but didn't fill my head with false hope. It was devastating when the doctor told me that I'd never walk again. That thought echoed through my mind, over and over, like a broken record player. I knew it was a long shot to walk again; but, if there was anything I could do to make it happen, I was going to do it.

When I arrived at St. Michael's, they told me that I would have a few days to relax and get settled in my new home away from home. After those few days, I would begin my rehab assignment. I was overwhelmed by the amount of core strength I had lost. I was unable to sit up for any length of time. If I was out of my hospital bed, I was required to wear a brace. The brace was in two pieces and had a hard shell. The front and back pieces would Velcro together and once on it looked like body armor. I felt like Robocop. The brace was awfully hot. I sweated like crazy while wearing it.

The day finally came the start of rehab. The nurses brought in my breakfast and told me that the therapist would be up shortly to begin my rehab. I finished my breakfast and right on cue, in came the therapist. He wheeled me down to the fitness center where the long road to recovery would begin. The first exercise he had me do was with this pulley system. I would have to pull down on a rope, similar to a close grip lat pull down movement. I reached up and pulled down. Immediately, I stopped after the first pull. The therapist inquired, "everything okay?" I had literally just shit myself.

The therapist quickly wheeled me back up to my room. From there the nurses would clean me up. I was humiliated and completely emasculated. Here I was, a grown man, and I couldn't even wipe my own ass. That's how my first day of rehab went. Not a great start but thankfully things would get much better.

Most people don't realize that the loss of bowel control accompanies most spinal cord injuries. The bowels are all affected by the nervous system and with mine being seriously compromised; it was completely out of my control. I had to use a catheter for a few weeks. When it came time to test out my bowel sensitivity, they removed the catheter to see if I would ever feel the urge to go. I never felt the urge. They looked at my bladder with an ultrasound, like they would with a pregnant mother to see her baby. They found that I was holding about 1200 cc's of fluid. Most people feel like they're about to pop around 600 cc's. I was left with two options.

I could go back to using the catheter or I could use what they call an "in and out." I told myself that there was no way I was using a catheter if it wasn't completely necessary. I decided to use the "in and out" before I even knew what it was. Each time I would have to urinate, typically twelve to fourteen times per day, I would have to put it in. Over the years, I've slowly regained bowel sensitivity and function. I can now go on my own but when my body says 'go,' I've got to go or there's going to be an accident.

I tried to get back to my normal routine as much as possible, while in the hospital. I requested that my therapy include some resistance training. The doctor's would decide against that idea but they couldn't prevent me from doing it on my own. I had a set of dumbbells right next to my bed and not too far from it, a tub of protein. I didn't care where I was; I knew where I was going.

I don't recall getting depressed during this time. I focused on what I needed to do and never lost hope. I tried to remain positive. Maybe it was because it hadn't fully clicked that being in a wheelchair would be my reality. Even if I did gain the ability to walk again, it wouldn't be like I use to. I had severe neurological damage that just couldn't be reversed. I kept the hope alive that I could get back to walking and standing, if only for a limited amount of time.

I did band therapy with the therapists and quickly started implementing resistance training with dumbbells. In an attempt to regain my ability to walk, I would be put in a harness that allowed me to stand up right. The harness would bare about ninety-five percent of my weight and the therapists would have to move my legs for me. This was an important part of the recovery process. It was critical that my brain and muscle attempt to reconnect and regain spatial awareness. Despite my effort, I saw very little progress relearning to walk. I wouldn't give up, though. But, I had a few other goals in my sites. They would help take my mind off of walking, as necessary.

Relearning how my body operates was quite the

challenge. When we learn to walk as kids, we don't really remember the process. I sure remember the process as an adult. Progress was slow and, at times, it seemed stagnant. It was as if I had gone from driving a Cadillac to an old, junky car. I wasn't functioning at a very high level.

I had to build up the feedback from the muscles in my legs and feet. Walking without this feedback to the brain was near impossible. Have you ever tried walking when your foot's asleep? You can hardly do it, can you? That's because your brain isn't getting the signal from the foot that your foot has moved. Our central nervous system (CNS) is constantly sending and receiving signals from the world around us. This allows us to move throughout our environment safely. I couldn't believe how much I had taken for-granted. When the CNS is compromised, it makes even the simplest of things difficult.

The human body is super complex. Doctors and therapists will tell you that there's a lot they know about nerves but there is still much to learn. The body is an intelligent creation and more capable and resilient than we often give it credit for. It's difficult to factor in a person's will and determination to succeed. The heart of a champion is hard to defeat. I truly believe that if you set your mind to something, the body will do whatever it can to allow you to succeed. The most successful people on the planet are full of determination and grit, willing to do whatever it takes in order to achieve their goals.

In flight school we had a saying, "Plan the flight. Fly the plan." I used this quote to fuel my recovery efforts.

"Plan the Flight. Fly the Plan."

Set a goal. Make a plan. Stick to the plan. If the plan fails, or obstacles arise, don't change your goal. Change the plan. Fix your approach. I aim to instill confidence and determination in everybody that I come across. Humans naturally want to resort to comfort zones and safety but there can be no growth in such places. It's counter-intuitive but safety zones can be danger zones, preventing one from reaching their true potential. Resistance is necessary and it makes you strong. There's a mindset necessary to endure the pain and struggle in order to achieve things. My goal is to get people to develop the proper mindset and realize that it is worth the hardship and difficulty.

I have made great strides in my life when I was pushed into a corner and forced to act. Forced-change can be a great motivator. You would be surprised what you can do when you have to. I know I was. I never knew my true potential until I was challenged. I never knew how strong I was until being strong was my only option.

I had made little progress with walking during rehab but I didn't allow that to stop my efforts. It was quite rare for somebody in my condition to be able to walk again. I didn't give much attention to the statistics. If I had anything to do with it, I would prove them wrong and walk again. I had to at least try. If I had never found the determination to try, I probably would have never walked again.

Once back home, I utilized the kitchen bar to help pull myself up. It was about waist level and I could lean on it with my forearms. Once up, I stood as long as I could without holding on. The first time I attempted I lasted three seconds. A few weeks later, I was up to five seconds. A few months later, I could stand for thirty seconds, then a minute, then five minutes. Albeit slow, I was pleased with the progress I was making.

I eventually progressed to a walker. It helped support about seventy-five percent of my weight, a big jump from the ninety-five percent that the contraption at the rehab center allotted for. Back at the station, I would have my own set up downstairs. It was just too difficult for me to get up and down the stairs. During my shifts, I would walk up and down the hallway. Two years of that and I would finally progress to forearm crutches. Each progression was slow and difficult. I knew that the process would be long and ugly. But, I was committed to walking again, no matter what it took. From forearm crutches, I progressed to a cane, where my progress would be the ugliest. I fell a lot with the cane, as I still had little to no feeling in my feet. Without that feeling, I had little spatial awareness. One moment I would be standing up, the next I'd be searching for the nearest thing to grab in an attempt to catch my fall.

After one of my falls, I recalled my visit to Rome in 2003. During this time, my hope was fading and I was beginning to think that I might not ever walk again. I remembered walking the streets of Rome and the Vatican City. Walking in a place with such history was inspiring and difficult to explain. I had purchased a set of wooden rosary beads, hand-crafted by local street merchants.

One of the places we explored was St. Mary's Cathedral. It is thought to have been built sometime between the years of 432 – 440 A.D. Despite a brutal earthquake in 1348, it still retains much of the core structure. I was amazed to see such an old building with such beauty and power within the walls. I walked around in pure amazement. I noticed that the details in several paintings were etched with pure gold. It was a very solemn and holy place.

In one of the rooms, aside the main sanctuary, I saw a priest. The thought came to my mind to have the rosary beads blessed. I managed to convince the priest to bless my beads, although he didn't speak any English. He anointed them and said a blessing over them in Italian. He finished the blessing by sprinkling Holy Water over them. The whole thing was pretty cool to watch.

The recovery from my accident had been brutal. There were many times were I badly struggled. I'd find myself lying on the floor, after a fall from the bar or crutches. This one particular instance, the wooden rosary beads came to mind. I hadn't thought much of them after packing them up for the return trip from Rome. I can't tell you why that I thought of them at this particular moment. Maybe I was running low on hope. Was I working toward an impossible goal? The beads were blessed in a holy city. Maybe they could help me out, I thought. I was willing to let anything aid my efforts. I had hit a trying time and had nowhere else to turn. I wasn't sure where the beads were but I was determined to find them.

I looked everywhere, all the kitchen drawers and every corner of every closet. I tore the house a part but finally, I found the beads. Once I found them, I remember gripping them so tight that they left an imprint on my palms. With tears in my eyes, I prayed that if it be God's will, to please allow me to walk once again. I cannot fully describe what happened in the next moments. An incredible sensation poured over me. The feeling started in my fingers and hands. It ran up my arms into my shoulders and then throughout my entire body.

I kept the beads nearby after that moment. Whenever I felt like walking again was too difficult, I'd look to the beads and know that it was in God's hands. The beads gave me an indescribable peace. As long as I continued to stay the course, God's will would be done. I consider it one of my greatest blessings that the Lord saw it fitting to allow me to walk again. Almost a year later, from saying that prayer with the beads, I was able to walk without any assistance.

I desperately wish that I knew where the beads were now. Over the years, they have been misplaced. However, I'll never forget their significance and symbol of hope. It's funny how such a small thing like rosary beads can play such an important role in our lives. The beads in and of themselves didn't do anything magical. But, they gave me hope. They pushed me to carry on when I wanted to doubt myself. Such things you just can't put a value on.

Surprisingly, my ability to walk has not been received well from everybody. I suppose no matter what you overcome or do there will always be people to hate on you. These days I get some things said behind my back about my ability to walk, although it's ugly at best and I have zero stamina. From time to time, I'll take pictures and video of me standing. Heck, sometimes I'll even go to the gym without my wheelchair. I take great pride in being able to walk again.

I think the hate mostly stems from a lack of knowledge about spinal cord injuries. Like most things, spinal cord injuries are not black and white. There are a lot of gray areas and I fall right in the middle. My injury is not a complete tear, although it's close. I have lost ninety percent of my neuron messaging ability and can send and receive very little input from brain to lower extremities. I do retain some feeling and function in my hips and that's what allows me to walk.

On occasion, you can find me in the gym without my wheelchair but it's not a pretty sight. I can get around from benches to machines fairly well. I've certainly taken a number of falls in the gym. I should probably always have my chair with me but I can still be a bit hardheaded. I suppose some things never change. I will say this, and I think it goes for anybody who's lost and then regained their ability to walk, I'm damn proud that I can walk again, no matter how weird it looks.

Some people have said that I'm just faking the dependency on my wheelchair for attention. I would get rid of my wheelchair in a heartbeat, if I could. If I had the ability to train legs, to squat and dead lift again, you bet your ass I would. But, as it is today, I can limp my way around the house and the gym. I can stand for a short amount of time.

You're crazy if you think I'm not going to get out of my chair every opportunity I get. Most people have no clue what I've had to go through, the struggle and adversity I've stared in the face and beat back. It's easy to judge from the comfort of an armchair but walk a day in their shoes before you pass judgment. Or, better yet, let the man who is without sin be the first to cast a stone.

I've accepted my situation for what it is. You won't find me sitting around feeling sorry for myself or trying to convince anybody else to feel sorry for poor, pitiful Chad. Most people will never know or appreciate all the struggle and adversity I've had to overcome. That's all right. I don't wish my situation on anybody. I'm also hesitant to pass judgment without knowing the full story. Heck, I do my best to avoid criticizing anybody!

I know that I am far from perfect. I think my story illustrates that clearly. If it hasn't done so yet, just wait. I don't try to be perfect. I embrace my shortcomings but I also celebrate my victories. If being able to walk, no matter how ugly or short-lived it is, isn't a victory, I'd like to know what the hell is. Realize that your path will be filled with critics and naysayers. Pay them little attention. They talk about you because they feel insufficient in their own endeavors. Your success acts like a spotlight on their missed opportunities. At times, I let the critics get the best of me. But, I'll never let them stop me or my mission. My story and life has become much greater than myself.

Walking again when others were convinced that it was impossible is one of the biggest accomplishments of my life. The things that are often the most difficult are also the most rewarding. I have a great sense of pride in my ability to walk.

It was a long and difficult journey but I'm sure glad that I took it.

CHAPTER EIGHT

"From a Chair"

Nothing about my life was designed to handle a wheelchair. The house wasn't set up for it. My job wasn't set up for it. My car dang sure wasn't accommodating. It was quite the transition. Being stuck to a wheelchair affected everything about my life. It seemed that each day that passed made me aware of new challenges. These new challenges were things I easily over looked. Simple tasks like getting dressed and leaving the house now required much more effort. It became frustrating at times.

"Normal" Life From a Chair

I remember the first time I sat on the toilet at home; I nearly fell in the thing. My legs had lost so much fat and muscle due to the inability to move. I looked down at my scrawny, pitiful legs and couldn't help but feel discouraged. All those hours in the gym, training my legs had been for nothing. I had nothing to show for all my hard work.

I had to get a completely new wardrobe. The pants I had no longer fit. My new wardrobe would consist of mostly wind pants and sweat pants. They were more comfortable and much easier to put on than a pair of blue jeans. To this day, you'll hardly see me in a pair of jeans. They just don't seem to fit right and are much less comfortable than my dress slacks.

Relying on the wheelchair for everything was a huge pain. To go anywhere was a big production. I had to pop the wheels off the chair, fold the chair, put the chair in the trunk of the car, and figure out how to manipulate the wheels so that they would fit. It was like real life Tetris. After getting the chair in the car, I had to figure out how to get myself in there. The whole process made me not want to leave the house unless I absolutely had to.

Things didn't get easier once I got out of the house. Handicap parking was frustrating. The American Disability Act was supposed to make things easier for those who are disabled. However, there's not a lot of enforcement or regulation of those rules. Many buildings aren't even compliant with the ADA. Most wheelchair ramps are too steep and walkways are too narrow.

Working From a Chair

My career as a firefighter and paramedic was over. When I went back to work, Red River wasn't exactly sure what to do with me. They put me in dispatch until they could figure something out. I worked in dispatch, answering calls and relaying messages to first responders. I can't say that I was overly enthusiastic about this position but I knew that I probably wouldn't stay there long. I had a feeling that they would move me somewhere else and do what they could to accommodate my situation.

After two years of working dispatch, they gave me a couple of choices. I could either take my disability or take a position that had opened up in the legal department. Taking a disability check never appealed to me. What the heck would I do all day? I've never been one to just sit around and do nothing. I decided to take the job with legal, knowing full well it would be a big change.

Before taking the position, I told them that I didn't want to stare at stack of papers all day long. They assured me that I wouldn't be doing that. But, I would have to go back to school and get certified as a paralegal. Great, after several years of EMT and paramedic classes, I would have to go back to school. I certainly wasn't thrilled about that but I did what I needed to do and earned my certification. I have been in that same office since 2007 and have served over seventeen years with the federal government.

I work as a paralegal specialist for the Department of Defense (non active) for the JAG office. Military lawyers are called Staff Judge Advocates. They abbreviate it J.A.G. Lawyers are hired by the government to write up proposals, acquisitions, contracts, any legally binding document. Companies and individuals, in the private sector, make bids on different projects that the government needs done.

Most of what I do is geared around research. I ensure that any proposals, acquisitions, and contracts comply with the rules and regulations of the governing body. I will research the regulations of the different military branches. It is my job to make sure that everything is legally sufficient. I am not the only one who ensures everything is legal, however. I am just one piece to the legal puzzle. The commander will consult with his legal team to make sure that everything is done properly and for the appropriate reason. The system is in place to keep everyone out of trouble.

Occasionally, people will try to sue the government, for whatever reason. In which case, I'll research the circumstances surrounding the case issues. The office I work in handles a wide range of tasks. We will also handle wills, power of attorneys, special power of attorneys, and much more, for deployed service members.

Like I said previously, my job is on the research side of things. When somebody needs to know whether something is legal to do, I provide them with the necessary information. I give them regulations surrounding their questions, along with the options they have to move forward with. I stay mostly in front of a computer all day. If I'm not on a computer, I'm on the phone talking to commanders or lawyers. I receive calls from all over but none grab my attention quite like calls from the Pentagon.

I never saw myself doing this type of work. Sitting at a desk all day never really suited my fancy but I consider myself blessed to still be able to work. Although my work is different now, than being a paramedic, it's still helpful and necessary work. Red River produces Bradley Tactical Vehicles, Humvees, and Mine-Resistant Ambush Protected (MRAP) vehicles. The MRAP vehicles have a bottom much like a boat. Instead of a flat bottom, it has a 'V' shaped undercarriage. This allows for the force (of an explosion) to be redirected to outside the vehicle, rather than the flat bottom absorbing all the impact. The MRAP is designed to withstand IED explosions. Its invention has saved hundreds of lives. Red River also provides a rubber product that aids in the repair of tires, on various types of tires. It's a specialty service that no other depots do. It can't be easily outsourced.

Red River Army Depot is an important part in our defense system. The supplies built at this depot are invaluable and have greatly supported our troops. I am proud that I have a small role in that aid. Red River is also responsible for bringing thousands of jobs to Northeast Texas. I know many people who work on base. Red River is a vital part to our local community as well as our global defense. It's a real honor to be a part of RRAD.

Bodybuilding From a Chair

Six months after my accident I was back on the bodybuilding stage. This time I competed as a wheelchair competitor. I had worked relentlessly to gain back all of the muscle I had lost after my accident. Prepping for competition took my mind off of my situation and allowed me a singular focus point. It gave me something to work towards. In September of 2005, I would be back on the Heart of Texas stage and this time the outcome would be much different.

I took home first place. My view on bodybuilding once again shifted. There was no way I would be able to compete with the monsters of the able-body division. But, as a wheelchair competitor, I would be much more competitive. In fact, I would never place worse than second in any shows. I was beginning to get accustomed to weight training from a wheelchair. Rolling around the gym and moving from bench to machine got easier and easier. Things were different now. I didn't stand quite so tall but things were brightening up, as far as bodybuilding was concerned. I had a real chance to become a professional bodybuilder. I ingrained earning my pro card into my brain. Every action would map towards that goal.

In 2006, I placed first at the Lone Star Challenge in Dallas. The very next year, I placed first in Little Rock at the Arkansas State Championships. I would also win the overall best poser award. That award included all classes, wheelchair and able body. I don't really think too much about my trophies. They serve as reminders of accomplishments I've achieved and the hard work it took to get there. I'd hardly say that they are 'prize possessions.' But, if I had to pick one that I was the most proud of, it would be the overall poser award

I won in Little Rock. Winning that award encouraged me to think bigger about my bodybuilding career. After all, I still had my sites on potentially winning my pro card. In 2008, I decided to compete in Wheelchair Nationals. My focus was on two things: work and getting ready for the national stage.

* * * * * * *

I've always looked to others for inspiration. As I said, figures like Rocky and Super Man inspired me when I was younger. As an adult, I found motivation elsewhere. During my prep for Wheelchair Nationals, I was introduced to a young lady named Fallon Turner. She worked out at the same gym I did so naturally our paths crossed. She had Cerebral Palsy, a disease that affects body movement and muscle coordination. But, her condition didn't stop here at all.

She was diving into the bodybuilding arena and I volunteered to help her train. I'm not sure she knew this but Fallon had been a big motivator in my life. I watched her defeat every obstacle in her way. I wanted to see her do the same in bodybuilding and wanted to help out if possible. It was my way to give back for what she had given to me.

As it would turn out, Fallon's mother was an editor for the Four States Magazine. She came to me and asked me if I'd be interested in sharing my story. This was the first time anybody had really inquired about my story. I told her that I'd be happy to share. Before I knew it, I was taking pictures and being interviewed for the article. The article hit many of the high points of my story and life after my injury. It was a great blessing but the real blessings had yet to come.

I was in Wal-Mart one afternoon, in line waiting to check out when I was approached by an older woman. She asked if I was the one featured in the Four States Magazine article. "Yes ma'am." I told her. She began telling me the story of her daughter and the rough times she was facing. She was going through a divorce and had recently lost her job. She was headed into a downward spiral. I wasn't exactly sure where this lady was going with this story but I listened intently.

The lady went on to tell me that her daughter had read my story in the Four States Magazine and became very inspired. She began to turn things around and got her life back together. I was not prepared to hear this. I was at a lost for words, which is rare for me. I don't recall how I responded to hearing that story but it served as another pivotal moment for me. It confirmed the need and impact of sharing my story could potentially have on others. As a paramedic, I was use to saving lives in traumatic situations. When this woman shared this story about her daughter, I realized that I was still able to save lives. My method would no longer be defibrillation paddles or advanced airway techniques. Rather, it would be by sharing my story.

I was highly motivated during this time of my life. I had gotten much of my spark back. Working with Fallon had turned up the bodybuilding motivation. I believe we fed off of each other and pushed each other to be better. Relationships like that can make your life exponentially better. I decided to go after that pro card full speed.

I showed up in West Palm Beach, FL with a soaring confidence. I had prepped for this show for eight months and did everything just as I needed to. There were some guys at the show that looked great. It was awesome meeting and getting to know them during the show. They have since become good friends and more motivation for me to keep moving forward. My confidence remained high and I felt good about my chances returning to Texas with professional status.

It played out differently in reality. I would not return with my pro card. I would finish second, missing the mark by one placing. I needed a first place finish in order to turn pro. I was bitter about this. Not that the guy who won hadn't earned it. He looked great and it was well deserved. I believe that I worked hard enough to earn it. I let myself down. I was also bitter about the fact that they only award one pro card. The able body divisions give out pro cards much more generously. The whole situation was a tough pill to swallow.

I didn't bounce back from this show like I should've. I allowed myself to get down and feel sorry for myself. My harsh reality was setting in. I could no longer ride motocross. I couldn't fly. My paramedic career was over. I had lost my identity and was struggling to find my place. I began to look for answers in all the wrong places.

Answering The Call

CHAPTER NINE

"The Dark Times"

I was bitter about how the 2008 Wheelchair Nationals had turned out. I had put my all into that show, just like all the ones before. But, I came up short, yet again. I can't say whether that was the initial catalyst or the straw that broke the camel's back. Regardless, it certainly didn't help matters. I found myself, once again, struggling to find my identity. I suppose the shock and awe had worn off and what was now normal just didn't sit well with me. I was in a bad place and my mind was plagued with dark emotions.

No longer could I have that sense of fulfillment working as a paramedic. I couldn't jump in a plane and fly anymore. My bodybuilding had been drastically altered. I had gone through a divorce. Murphy's Law was ever-present. My world had been completely shaken and the dust was beginning to settle. I was coming to realize that this was my reality. It's true that life goes on whether you are ready for it or not.

I find it strange that it took several years for this to happen. Perhaps, my preoccupation with bodybuilding resulted in this delay. I was now forced to face the music and deal with my reality. My life had become boring; I was complacent. My life before the accident was filled with adrenaline pumping activities like motocross, flying an airplane, and responding to emergencies. It was a huge paradigm shift. Now, I sat at a desk all day and stared at a computer screen. I looked forward to the gym. The gym was all I had but it would also become boring. It was becoming hard for me to see the purpose of it all.

The past three years I had used painkillers. I didn't need them much after the first year post injury, but I couldn't get off of them. I had become too reliant on them. My body craved them. I was addicted and slightly abusive of them. The painkillers helped me escape my reality. If only temporarily, they made everything better or, at least, minimized my care. I managed to cut the addiction before it got too out of hand. I decided to get some help and checked into rehab.

At the time, Shreveport had a well-known rehab center. I found it kind of ironic that I would be going back to Shreveport, where I spent several weeks after my injury. I was going to need all the help I could get. Statistics show that ninety-five percent of people are unable to break the addiction without medical help. I remember filling out what seemed to be an endless amount of paper work. Things got really strange when they had me take my belt and shoelaces off. Then, they duct-tapped my shoes to my feet. "What in the hell have I gotten myself into?!"

The nurses walked me through several sets of doors that required a code and buzzed before opening. We arrived in this waiting room like place. I saw people in handcuffs; some were reading magazines, and this one older lady with an unlit cigarette in her mouth continuously running into the wall. I didn't sit there long before I walked up to the front desk.

"I think I'm in the wrong place." I told the lady behind the glass.

"I'm sorry Mr. McCrary but you're not allowed to leave." She responded.

"Well, I checked myself in here. Why can't I check myself out?" I said in rebuttal.

She handed me a form and said that if I filled it out, I could leave in seventy-two hours.

"Seventy-two hours?!" I exclaimed. "There's no way I'm staying here that long."

"I'm afraid that's all we can do, Mr. McCrary." She said as she politely closed the window.

A slight panic filled me. I tried to remain calm and rely on my problem solving skills. A little while later, I was sitting outside in what seemed to be a prison yard. It sure felt like it. I felt like Andy Duphrane when he first arrived at Shawshank. As I observed around the outside area, I noticed some workers who were bringing in materials to repair some floors. I watched him closely to see if I could pick up any habits that I could take advantage of. The thought came to my head that maybe I could sneak out of this place.

When I was back inside, I noticed one worker coming up to my floor. I noticed that the doors allowed entry only with a key code. I studied his routine and had it down. The next time he would come, I would sneak past him. He opened the door and I snuck passed without him seeing me. I raced down the stairs. It was hard to believe that I didn't fall; it had to have been one ugly site to see. I didn't much care. I just wanted to get out.

When I arrived at the bottom of the staircase, I was met by two guards. I told them, confidently, that I was part of the floor installation crew. They didn't buy it. "What's that on your wrist?" one of the guards asked. I had forgotten about my impatient bracelet and the fact that my shoes were duct tapped to my feet. "Look, I'm getting out of here one way or another. We can do this the easy way or the hard way." I said, as adrenaline was pumping through my veins. "Do what you gotta do man." One of the guards said, as they both turned the other way.

I managed to get across the street to the funeral home next door. I called a buddy, told him the whole story, and convinced him to come pick me up. While at the funeral home, I was met by the director of the rehab center. He had no authority to send me back, as I wasn't under any court order to be there. I checked myself in. I could tell that he wanted to talk. I assumed that he was going to attempt to convince me to come back across the street. But, he didn't. He wasn't mad or outraged. He was more intrigued on how I escaped.

"It's quite obvious that you're not coming back. I'm not here to convince you to do so, either. Rather, I'm curious to hear how you managed to escape. I've been running this rehab center for over twenty-one years and I've never had a single person escape." He said.

I told him the story and then made my way down the street to the convenient store where I told my buddy to pick me up. He picked me up and carried me home. I managed to get off of painkillers on my own, a near impossible feat by looking at the numbers. I suppose I just wanted it bad enough. As bad, or even more so, as I wanted to escape from that rehab center. I would no longer be burdened by my addiction of painkillers but a new enemy would surface. This one would turn out to be even more difficult to defeat.

* * * * * * *

When I started taking classes to become a paramedic, I completely quit drinking. It was something I did for entertainment before changing my career path to become a paramedic. My new journey didn't require it so I did away with it. I also thought that my patients deserved to have me at my best. I couldn't afford to give patients any less than one hundred percent. Things were serious and the stakes were high.

I had my first drink in over a decade at the age of thirty-nine. I started dating a girl who enjoyed the occasional glass of wine. I decided that an occasional glass wouldn't hurt anything. After all, I was no longer working as a paramedic. Heck, the glass of wine even did some good. My feet would shake from time to time due to the nerve damage. The glass of wine alleviated that. I figured that this small, occasional consumption wouldn't affect me at all.

I would've been right if I would've stayed with the small, occasionally consumption. One glass of wine a night quickly turned into two, then three, then four. Within eight months, I had completely stopped going to the gym and was drinking an entire box of wine every day. It had gotten so bad that I would have withdrawals without regular consumption.

I remember waking up one morning to find that I didn't have any wine in the house. I rummaged through the kitchen, the living room, my bedroom, everywhere. There was none to be found. My mind then turned to the bathroom where I found a bottle of rubbing alcohol. I had no choice but to drink it and relieve the symptoms of withdrawal.

A week later, I found myself in an even worse place. I drank myself into oblivion. I was too far-gone, I told myself. There would be no saving me or coming back from this. Once again, I was in a deep, dark place. Thinking back on this time in my life sends chills down my spine. I felt useless… hopeless. I figured that I would do society a favor and end it all. I had messed up my life in that stupid accident. Now, I was just a burden to society. I had made up my mind. There was only one thing to do.

On November 3rd, 2014, I grabbed my pistol, loaded the chamber, and began to crawl out my back door and down the steps. I decided that I would take to the woods, in hopes that nobody would find me. I also didn't want to make a mess in the house. That's how crazy my mind had gone. I crawled hundreds of feet, on my stomach, like a solider through a hostile battlefield. I went through vines and thorns until I found a small clearing, which looked suitable for my final moments. I looked around and caught a glimpse of my legs. They had been scrapped and cut by the underbrush of the woods. My legs lay in a bloody mess. I wasn't too much bothered by this finding. What I was about to do was going to be much worse.

I pulled the hammer back on the pistol. I pulled the gun up to my head. The cold steel rested slowly but firmly against the side of my head. Everything seemed to be in slow motion. The blink of my eyes would take several seconds. The beat of my heart was forceful but slow. The woods whispered, "You don't have to do this. You don't have to do this." But, the decision was made. I closed my eyes one final time.

Answering The Call

CHAPTER TEN

"One Final Recovery"

Many think that suicide is a selfish act. I would disagree. I decided that it was my only option because I felt like I had nothing left to offer. I thought I would be doing society a favor. I felt like I was in the way, a burden to society. Everywhere I went I drew attention and required special accommodation. I hated that. I just wanted to be like every one else. If you've never been on the edge of suicide, you don't know what would motivate somebody to make that decision. It's a complicated issue. I think it's unfair to simply declare it selfish. You have to be in a dark place to have yourself convinced that suicide is the only option.

Three days later, I woke up in the Intensive Care Unit. I could hear people moving around me and the familiar beeps from a cardiac monitor. All of these things were far too familiar. I had been in similar situation a few years before. I received bad news then and I assumed that things weren't too good now. A few minutes would pass before I realized the circumstances. My last memories of lying in the woods came to mind. My first thought was that my suicide attempt had failed. I slowly raised my hand up to my head, scared to see how much of it remained. I let out a huge sigh of relief when I realized that my head was still all there.

Several days later I would find out that I passed out due to alcohol poisoning. I had never pulled the trigger. In that hospital bed, I decided that I would get some help. I toyed with the idea that I was still here for a reason. Once I had recovered enough to leave the hospital, I decided that it would be necessary for me to go to rehab. I needed to get clean for good. I would go to Camden, AR. Home of one of the top rehab centers in the country.

The doctors told me that I was in pretty bad shape. This wasn't news to me. I knew how bad things had gotten. At this point, I just wanted to get well. The first week of detox was miserable. I remember late at night sitting on the side of my bed, shaking violently. I went several days without sleep. When I did manage to fall asleep, it would only last a few hours. It was a miserable existence. I couldn't sleep. I couldn't eat. It was next to impossible to get my mind of the pain.

I did my best to commit this suffering to memory. No way I was going to get myself in this position again. It was time to get my life together and make something of myself once again. I was given a second chance. I had no intentions of wasting it. The disciplined lifestyle of bodybuilding had been my saving grace in the past. It would turn out to save me once again.

I quickly got back into my old lifting and eating routine. I accompanied that with Alcoholic Anonymous (AA) meetings, once a week. The first step of their twelve-step program is admitting that you have a problem. I had no problem admitting that. The pain and suffering from detoxing was more than enough to convince me that I never needed another drink of alcohol. I believe that was a big key to my success of getting clean. I never tried to lie to myself or attempt to convince myself that nothing was wrong and that I'd be fine. I knew that was a lie. My rehab experience confirmed it.

I haven't had a drop of alcohol since dragging myself to the woods that day. I might be able to handle a drink now. But, I'll take no chances of a relapse and returning back to that dark place. I don't desire it anymore, anyway. It's kind of like a kid who eats so much of his favorite candy that he gets sick of it and never wishes to eat it again. I look at things very differently thanks to my rehab experiences. I consider whether or not something is going to add value to my life before I decide to partake. I think that's a good lens to see life through.

I prefer to have a small circle of friends, whom I can rely on at any given moment. I enjoy my gym time and speaking with others about training and nutrition. I get really excited when I get the opportunity to share my story with others. To me, it doesn't matter if I'm speaking to 800 people or just one. I've seen the impact of sharing my story. It's powerful and that probably surprises me more than it does anybody else. It's crazy and humbling. I wish I would have realized it sooner than I did. It has always been a great joy to be able to help others.

CHAPTER ELEVEN

"Back on Stage"

    I would've never anticipated that learning to walk again would haunt me in the future. After the 2016 national show, there was some talk about competitors with partial spinal cord injuries. There was questioning whether it would be fair to let them compete. Did they have an unfair advantage if they were able to walk, even if it was intermittently? I was worried that they would rule against partial spinal cord injuries and not allow me to compete. If that were to happen, there would be little I could do and no other division for me to compete in. I would have no choice but to hang my hat on my bodybuilding career.

Answering The Call

The first two months of 2017 had gone well. I had several opportunities to speak and share my story. My preparation for the March show had been smooth. I was bigger and leaner than last year, which is the goal of every competitive bodybuilder. I was right on track to earning my pro card. I had put my all into this show and had high hopes that this was my year.

As the show drew nearer, I was feeling better and better. 2017 would be my year. I was certain that I'd finally be able to check off achieving professional bodybuilding status. I wasn't too worried about becoming pro for the benefits. I wanted it because it was a goal I had set a long time ago. When I set out to achieve it, I knew that it would take years of hard work and discipline. It was the journey that would make the pro card special. There's not a whole lot of benefit to being a professional bodybuilder, despite what social media would have you believe. I didn't do it for the fame or to get a supplement deal. I did it for me. I did it because I wanted to.

In 2016, I had placed first in the heavyweight and masters division. But, it was the controversial second place finish in the overall that made me hungrier than ever. Having the taste of victory in front of my face was brutal. I used that to fuel my training for the 2017 show. I didn't want a repeat of last year. It was within my grasp and this year would be the year that I'd reach out and grab it.

The week leading up to the show is commonly referred

to as "peak week," in the industry. It's critical to have your timing down with food (mainly carbs) and water so that when you step on stage you look your very best. A lot of competitors do some crazy stuff during this week. In my early and inexperienced bodybuilding days, I feel victim to some crazy recommendations, as all competitors do when they're starting out. I've competed enough now to keep things simple and effective.

For the most part, my peak week went smoothly. But, typical of life, there can be some unexpected surprises pop up that require you to handle them. Thursday of peak week I was thrown for a loop. Just two days before the competition I received a phone call.

"Yes, is this Chad McCrary?" a familiar sounding voice said. I recognized the voice but couldn't quite put my finger on who it was.

"Yessir, this is Chad," I responded. After my response, it clicked and I knew exactly who I was talking to.

"I'm afraid I have some bad news. Unfortunately, you have been disqualified from competing this weekend."

"What?!" I asked in disbelief.

"Well, we have received a video of you walking around the gym. We feel like you may have an unfair advantage over the other competitors."

The video he was referencing was one on my website. I had filmed a workout with Nick LaToof at Legend's Gym. Some of the shots you can see me standing up but the video failed to capture any clips of me actually walking. If you could see me walking, it would be very evident that I had no such advantage by hobbling around the gym. As I've stated before, I'm unable to train legs. I can stand and walk for only a few minutes at a time.

The voice continued, "we do plan on paying you back for your airfare and hotel. We'd still like you to come and guest pose."

I sat there in utter disbelief. I reluctantly agreed and told him that I'd be there and hung up the phone. After the call, I sat in silence, not quite able to believe everything that had just happened. Was this real? Was there anything I could do?

I called my doctor and told him what had just transpired. I asked him if there was anyway he could send over my MRI's and his opinion on my injuries. After all, my condition had always been accepted by the WCBB (Wheelchair Bodybuilding). I didn't expect the gesture to change anything but it certainly couldn't hurt.

I felt wronged and I wasn't the only one who thought so. I shared the news with friends and family via social media.

People have shown interests in following my journey so I try to keep them up to date with everything that's going on. Several of my friends and followers were upset with the ruling. Heck, some of them probably more upset than I was. If you believe that there's a silver lining to every cloud, the silver lining here was all the support I received. I didn't realize that so many people cared and followed my journey. It really meant a lot to me and still very much does.

My mindset had shifted dramatically. My mental preparation changed from competition to guest posing. I was angry and frustrated by the whole thing. I didn't sign up to guest pose; I signed up to win the damn show. I knew that I would have a target on my back coming into this show but I never knew that it would lead to something like this.

I stayed strict with my diet and water manipulation just in case that something would change and I would be able to compete. I still wanted to look my best on stage, guest posing or competing. I kept a small hope that the ruling would be changed. I did my best to make the most of the situation but it was difficult to keep my focus. I told myself that I should at least enjoy a free vacation to Florida.

Murphy's Law would strike again, as I began my travel itinerary. My flight from Texarkana on Thursday evening was cancelled causing me to miss my connection in Dallas. In order for me to get back on track with my travel schedule, I would need to drive to Little Rock early Friday morning. If that flight went according to schedule it would still put me in West Palm Beach by noon on Friday.

Traveling for me is already stressful enough. Throw in water manipulation and cancelled flights and it makes everything even more interesting. Fortunately, the rest of the trip went smoothly. I arrived in the sunshine state just after noon. I decided that I would try to relax and get my mind off of everything that had taken place over the last twenty-four hours. I grabbed a steak and sweet potato at a restaurant just down the street from my hotel. Afterwards, I made my way up to my room to relax.

Around 9:00 PM, my phone rings. "Hey Chad," the show promoters voice echoed through the phone. "We've been doing a lot of thinking and ummm…"

There was hesitation in his voice, like a kid who knew he was in trouble but refused to admit it.

"We feel that our ruling was unfair… we've decided to allow you to compete tomorrow."

"That's great news." I replied with a monotone voice. "I'll see you in the morning."

I thought the timing of this call was telling. He must've put this phone call off as long as he could. His voice sounded a bit reluctant, like he knew that he needed to reinstate me but didn't want to.

"And Chad, let's keep this off of social media. Okay?"

"Sure." I replied and hung up the phone.

He had assured me that this would have no affect on the outcome of the show. I couldn't help but roll my eyes at that. There was then, and still is now, no doubt that all of this played a role in determining the outcome. Think about it. It would've raised quite the fuss if I were to win. A competitor on the verge of getting disqualified winning the whole show. It certainly would've raised some questions.

I showed up the next morning and did my thing. I hit all of my poses and felt good about things despite all the happenings leading up. There was a lingering suspicion of no matter how well I did; my fate had already been determined. I felt like they had already written me off. If I were to win the show it would only spark more controversy. I didn't stand a chance.

I went on to finish in second place. Both, in the heavyweight and master divisions. I didn't even qualify for the overall. I saw this coming from a mile away and wasn't surprised at all. Second place was a good spot for me to finish. A pro card for me was out of the question, in the judge's eyes. But, they knew better than to push my placing any further down. After all, bodybuilding is a very subjective sport. It wouldn't be difficult to point out a few things that allowed one guy to beat me. I'm not knocking the guy who placed first. He had a great physique and deserved it. I knew he had worked just as hard as I did.

I didn't put up much of a fuss. I was over it. This show had left a bad taste in my mouth, much worse than the previous year. I just wanted to get out and enjoy some Florida sunshine for a couple of days. When I returned home, there was no doubt in my mind that my bodybuilding lifestyle would continue. The question of whether I would compete again was not so easily answered. Only time will tell. As of right now, I am not sure. I have little interest to compete. I love competing and the process but the 2017 show really sucked out all the fun for me. I don't have a good reason to get on stage anytime soon. I'm not saying that I won't but I can't promise that I will.

If I do decide to get back on stage, maybe I can bring home that pro card. It's one of the few goals I've set that I haven't been able to accomplish. I often wonder if it'll be a bitter sweet feeling, not unlike receiving my paramedic patch as I lay in my hospital bed. Achieving pro status doesn't have the same glory it once did. My desire has weakened for it. I'm confident that there are more fulfilling things to pursue.

I think I'll shift my priorities to something different, perhaps more impactful and something that I can be more proud of. One thing that this bodybuilding journey has taught me is that you should never underestimate the impact you have on others. Big or small, if you influence others, you should never take that for-granted. The support and feedback from the people in my life during this journey has been overwhelming. I am truly grateful for everyone who has stood by my side, even for those who no longer do so.

I never thought my story would be of such inspiration and motivation as it has proven to be. I have great conviction, now more so than ever, to share my story, whenever and however possible. That conviction led to the creation of this book. I know it will continue to lead to more things in the future. My prayer is that it helps those who find themselves down, facing horrible adversity to find hope and to realize that tough times never last but tough people do.

I've realized that this calling is much bigger than myself. I am being disobedient if I do not do what's necessary to share my story. It is for others that I share. I believe that it has become my calling and new platform that God has given me.

CHAPTER TWELVE

"Answering the Call"

Several times in my life I have felt strong convictions. That day sitting on my buddy's tailgate would turn out to be a pivotal moment. In 2008, I remember feeling like I needed to share my story. I ignored it but it resurfaced in 2010. It was harder this time but I managed to suppress that conviction as well. I didn't feel worthy to tell my story. What good would it do others? I was still trying to figure out my new place in this world. Eventually, the conviction would be too loud for me to ignore. I had no choice but to answer the call.

As ironic as it sounds, getting on stage in front of people never appealed to me. Who would want to come and listen to me? I know, I know. I get on stage in front of people when I compete in bodybuilding shows. That wasn't easy at first, either. It's also much different. The bright lights shining on you wash out the crowd. You can barely see the judges sitting right in front of the stage. Plus, I didn't have to say anything. All I had to do was walk out, hit my poses, smile and wave. That was fairly easy. I practiced it so much that it had become second nature.

However, I felt a strong conviction that I needed to start sharing my story. But, I just couldn't answer the question, who the heck am I? I was more qualified to tell you what you shouldn't do rather than give you advice on how to live your life. I wasn't qualified to be a life coach; I certainly wasn't trying to convince anybody that I was. Like Frank Zane said, "I'm no expert. I'm just an expert on me." Some days that conviction was as loud and present as the phone ringing. I refused to answer. I didn't want to do it. It would be very uncomfortable.

It's easy for us to resort back to our comfort zones. We feel safe there. It's familiar territory but no growth comes from those places. I knew this but refused to act upon this new calling. I hadn't put my complete trust and faith in God. I was reliant on my own abilities and remained unable to convince myself that I was capable of making an impact. I knew my story well. It wouldn't be a problem telling it. I just wasn't convinced that it would help anybody.

I've always had a passion for helping people. I answered the call to become a paramedic and firefighter and was able to help people each and every day of work. I had built up some credibility in the health and fitness space and was able to help people with their workouts and nutrition. I even earned my certified personal trainer (CPT) credential in order to help others better. Helping people is something I enjoyed doing. It was a way for me to give back.

In 2015, I felt the conviction once again. This time it was stronger than ever. I finally gave into it. What was the worst thing that could happen? I was extremely fortunate and blessed to have the people surrounding me with the knowledge and resources to help me out. I had a website built and flyers made. I began to advertise my story.

A few weeks went by, then a few months and nothing happened. I felt like Kevin Costner in *The Field of Dreams*. I'm sure we're all familiar with the famous line from the movie, "Build it and they will come." Ray (Kevin Costner's character) had destroyed several acres of precious crop to make a baseball field, lights and all. He spared no expense having no clue who would come.

Ray builds the field and no one comes, initially. He waits

and waits; all the while the critics call him crazy and insane. He gets frustrated, like anyone would, I suppose, in that situation. He answered the call and held up his end of the deal. Now it was time to get his return. Ray continued to wait and eventually famous baseball players of the past began to show up. "Shoeless" Joe Jackson, Archibald "Moonlight" Graham, and Buck Weaver were among the many ball players who would show and take the field, under the lights, once more.

Like Ray, I needed a bit more patience. I'll admit that I've never been the most patient person. I'm a go-getter. I enjoy making things happen. When I want something, I go after it, full speed. I get a little anxious when things are out of my control. But, God was in control. He always has been and always will be. That's something that this leap of faith has certainly taught me. Trust in Him and lean not on my own understanding.

I got asked to speak at the New Boston Rotary Club one evening. I wouldn't be paid. Instead, they provided me with some food. I agreed. It sounded like a sweet gig to me and the experience would be beneficial. There were only fifteen people there but there might as well have been fifteen thousand. I was so nervous and sweated profusely. I stumbled all over my words. To this day, I have no clue what I said. After I was finished, everyone stood up and clapped. Some even wanted to take pictures with me and ask me questions afterward. I must've said something good to get such a response. I didn't look much into it. I was just glad it was over.

I do recall one lady asking me if I believed that God allowed my injury to happen. I'm not sure how I responded then. If you were to ask me today, I'd say that it's incredibly difficult for humans to grasp the concept of God and His infinite wisdom. It's easy to wonder why things happen the way that they do and why there's so much evil in the world. "Why does God allow so much evil to exist?" I think it's an unfair question to ask.

We, as individuals, only have control over our actions and our responses to what happens around us. I'm not sure why evil exists. Maybe it's necessary so that we can appreciate the good. Perhaps, war is necessary so that we can confide in peace. I do know this: I don't know everything. The more that I do learn the more I realize how much I don't know. I don't have all the answers, nobody does. I will continue to put my faith and trust in God. He has the master plan and understands it far better than I do.

The speaking at the Rotary Club was the first speaking of many to come. The next one I do would be much bigger and very special. I had the great privilege of speaking at my old high school alma mater, DeKalb. I was nervous about this one. I spoke in front of the entire high school and middle school, which combined to be over 400 students. Initially, I had thought that maybe I made too big of a jump and bit off more than I could chew.

I'm not a speaker that plans out his entire speech. I make notes and practice speaking but I like to go with the flow and share what's on my heart. I know the story; heck, I lived it. I had a slideshow put together with some pictures of me before and after the accident. I told the story of how doctors said that I'd probably never walk again. I like to conclude that story by standing up out of my wheelchair and walking to the podium.

That part always gets a nice roar of applause and it fills me with great pride. With each off-balanced step, I'm reminded of the difficult journey I had to venture down in order to be able to walk again. It's powerful and I get emotional just thinking about it. I'm proud that I am able to walk a short distance. I truly believe that you can do anything that you set your mind to. I try to make that hit home with the students I share my message with. My life has been filled with accomplishing challenging feats and overcoming adversity. That was my message to those kids that day and remains my message today.

The feedback I got from those kids was incredible. Many students wanted to take a picture and chat with me. Some wanted my autograph. It was crazy. I could hardly believe it. Never in a million years would I have expected for this to be happening to me. My goal was to reach one, maybe two students and have them take to heart my message. I think that it's safe to say that my message reached several students that day.

I had several teachers come up to me and tell me how captivated the students were. They were normally a pretty rowdy bunch, I was told. I could certainly relate to that. I wasn't the most civilized student back in high school myself. Occasionally, I'll still have people talk to me about that day. It was an honor to be back in my old high school and speak to kids that walked the same hallways that I did. It'll be a day that I'll never forget.

It would be irresponsible for me to take all the credit. It may have been my story but it's far from my message. I'm just the medium for spreading the message. It's God's message. He just chose me to share it through. It really began to click for me that this was my new calling and something I needed to actively pursue. I had been given a new way to help people. More opportunities began to present themselves, each one bigger than the last.

I spoke to several schools in the Northeast Texas and Southwest Arkansas area. Each one had great turnouts and responses. Afterwards, the kids wanted autographs and pictures. I signed all sorts of crazy things from basketballs, tee shirts, hands, and even an iPhone. I double-checked to make sure he really wanted me to sign it. He was adamant so I did.

I was starting to think that I had seriously underestimated my story's impact. I wanted to kick myself for not realizing it sooner.

I've witnessed first hand the power of my story and the message it sends. But, it's still difficult for me to get it out there and allow people to hear it. Self-promotion is a tricky thing. It can come off conceited and self-centered. Usually, it's perceived that way by those who are jealous or maybe they just don't know the full story. I try my absolute best to let people know that it's not for my fame or glory. It's for God's glory. I ran from this calling for years. I didn't want it, for whatever reason. I'm simply being obedient and doing what I'm called to do. I answered the call.

The speaking's have slowed a bit, as of late. I've had several other things in the works, including this book, which I believed, that were necessary to prioritize. I'm convinced that my speaking is far from over and I will soon be back on stage once more. Heck, you may be reading this book after hearing one of my talks. In which case, I can't thank you enough for your time, attention, and support.

I've been so blessed with numerous people who surround my everyday life and have helped me get to where I am today. There's no way I'd be here without them. You'll never hear me say anything about being 'self-made.' No matter where you are in life, you've had people help you along the way. Every book you've read, person you've talked to, has somehow, someway shaped your thinking and ultimately, your life.

You may be reading this and thinking about the thing you've felt convicted to do. For whatever reason, you haven't started yet. You may be like me and not feel worthy or that it would be beneficial to anybody. I pray that you don't put off answering that call. I was lucky that the opportunity didn't pass me by before I was able to seize it. This book was another thing I was convicted to do. I thought about it for years but my ignorance to the process kept me from answering that call. Like I said previously, in God's timing I found myself surrounded by the right people with the right resources and the book was able to come to fruition.

It's a surreal feeling having my story in physical book form. It's another call that I have answered. Each time I have made the sacrifice to go after what my heart was telling me, it has been very rewarding. I look forward to seeing the fruits this book will produce. I have no doubts that it will inspire and motivate. It will reach people I never thought possible. I know this because it's not of my own doing. My story and life have become about something much bigger than myself.

CHAPTER THIRTEEN

"Overcoming Adversity"

Looking back on my life, there are a few common themes. I can point out specific moments in my life when I felt an indescribable conviction to make a change; to do something that I once thought was not possible. I took those leaps of faith and grew stronger and wiser with each one. I was never disappointed when I took those risks, although they required a tremendous amount of faith and hard work. It all seemed to work out just as it was meant to. I believe it does for everyone who truly follows their heart and chooses to go in the direction of their convictions.

With every chance you take in life, you're guaranteed to face adversity. Even if you play it safe, you'll face obstacles. No one is immune. Don't be surprised if you face barriers throughout your entire journey. Allow them not to discourage you. Many people will choose to walk in the direction of their dreams but most will never make it to their destination. They will quit at the first sign of adversity. But, that's not you. You are strong and powerful. These obstacles placed in your path are not in the way. Those obstacles become the way and prepare you for the next challenge.

I remember the day it clicked for me. I was at work, after my accident. It was just before 7:00 AM. We were changing shifts and I was about to head home. I had felt a desire to get a tattoo but I had no idea what I wanted or where I wanted to put it. Whatever the catalyst was that morning, I haven't a clue. But, for whatever reason, I discovered what tattoo I wanted.

I left work and went home. I made myself breakfast and patiently waited for the tattoo shop to open. I arrived at the place about five minutes before the shop opened. Once I saw them turn on the open sign and unlock the doors, I went inside. I told the guy that I wanted "Overcoming" on my right forearm and "Adversity" on my left forearm. I wanted it this way so that when I looked in the mirror I could read it. It would be there as a constant, permanent reminder of all the obstacles I had overcome. It was there also to encourage me that I was capable of overcoming any obstacles in the future. It's been a reminder to me ever since.

Much of my story is about overcoming adversity but that's not exclusive to me. Everyone goes through trying times. Those times and how your respond are usually what determine the course of your life. You can get bitter or you can get better. It's as simple as that.

I hope that my story can inspire and motivate. But, more so, I hope that your story can inspire and motivate. I'm no better than anybody. In fact, there's a good chance that you have more potential than I ever did. But remember, potential just means that you haven't done it yet. Refuse to believe anybody that tells you that you can't do something. Don't let anybody outwork you. Teach yourself to become resourceful. You don't have a lack of resources, despite what you may think. It may just be a lack of resourcefulness. Bet on yourself and be disciplined in your approach.

I have found no joy in climbing small mountains. But, the higher your goal, the higher the price tag. Make sure you know of the price to be paid for the things you want. Are you willing to pay it? I'm not talking about monetary payment. I'm talking about a payment in sacrifice. Hard work and relentless effort married with an extraordinary amount of patience. Nothing comes over night. Set your aim high and don't settle for less.

There will be plenty of times that you'll want to give up. There will be no shortage of people that encourage you to give up. Expect some of that encouragement to come from unlikely places, possibly from the people who are closest to you. Do your best to anticipate the unexpected and don't allow yourself to be surprised when crazy things happen. Manage your emotions. When things are going good, don't think it'll stay that way forever. The same thing goes for when things are going bad. This too shall pass. Keep your cool and stay focused. You're capable of great things. Allow yourself to believe that.

Stay Strong. Be Relentless.

"The human body is capable of amazing physical deeds. If we could just free ourselves from our perceived limitations and tap into our internal fire, the possibilities are endless."

- Dean Karnazes

ABOUT CHAD

[picture courtesy of the Texarkana Gazette]

Chad is a wheelchair bodybuilder, motivational speaker, and a paralegal specialist for the federal government. Chad's calling of helping others has taken several forms throughout his life. He once saved lives as a paramedic and firefighter. Now, Chad saves lives in a different way by sharing his powerful story and testimony of overcoming adversity.

Chad's overall mission is to help others. Whether that's sharing his story or giving people workout and nutritional advice. It doesn't much matter to Chad. He aims to use his platform and experience to motivate others to live their best life and go after the desires of their heart. Chad will be the first to tell you that there's nothing special about him. He just refuses to give up and accept what others think is impossible. May his story motivate and inspire you to achieve what others will tell you is impossible.

Answering The Call

ABOUT NICK

Nick is an author, speaker, and social influencer. He's well versed in the health and fitness industry after working for six plus years as a fitness professional. Nick's mission is to show people that it is possible to live life on your terms. He aims on debunking the common excuses and barriers most people claim are in their way. Nick encourages others to view things differently and ask better questions.

Nick's appetite for adventure and epic views have shaped his traveling lifestyle. Much like Chad, Nick aims to help people through his actions. You won't see him encouraging you to do anything that he hasn't done. He strives to best lead by example. Along his journey, he shares insights and thoughts about being in some of the most special places that this planet has to offer.

Answering The Call

The Christopher and Dana Reeve Foundation

Chad is a supporter and affiliate of the Christopher and Dana Reeve Foundation. The foundation is dedicated to finding cures and treatments for those affected by spinal cord injuries. Their mission statement reads:

> "The Reeve Foundation is dedicated to curing spinal cord injury by funding innovative research, and improving the quality of life for people living with paralysis through grants, information and advocacy."

Chad's love of Super Man was prevalent as a young kid. His infatuations lead him to ultimately pursue bodybuilding and learning to fly a plane. After his accident in 2005, Chad another thing in common with Super Man.

Christopher Reeve was the actor who Chad watched play the Super Man character in the 1978 film. Reeve would suffer a similar injury to Chad's, after being thrown from his horse during an equestrian competition in Virginia. Reeve would be confined to a wheelchair for the rest of his life. After Reeve's accident, he lobbied for those affected by spinal cord injuries. He contributed greatly to stem cell research and in 1982 founded the Reeve Foundation, now called the Christopher and Dana Reeve Foundation.

Chad's honored to be an affiliate and advocate for the foundation. Chad knows first hand the difficulties that those with spinal cord injuries face. A percentage of each book purchased will go to the Christopher and Dana Reeve Foundation to support spinal cord research.

Answering The Call

Chad McCrary

Christopher & Dana Reeve Foundation Copyright © 2017

Copyright © NickLaToof.com LLC

Answering The Call

More Information

To find out more about Chad, visit
http://www.chadmccraryinspires.com

Follow Chad online:

Facebook: Chad Russell McCrary

Instagram: @mccrarychad

To find out more about Nick, visit
http://www.nicklatoof.com

Follow Nick online:

Facebook: Nick LaToof

Instagram: @nlatoof

Twitter: @nlatoof

To find out more about the Christopher and Dana Reeve Foundation, visit https://www.christopherreeve.org

Facebook: Christopher & Dana Reeve Foundation

Instagram: @reevefoundation

Twitter: @reevefoundation

Answering The Call

Made in the USA
Coppell, TX
24 March 2022

75511225R00085